THE COMPLETE

WIN AT WHIST

Joseph D. Andrews

BARON BARCLAY
BRIDGE SUPPLY

05 04 03 02 01

Library of Congress Control Number: 00-109843
ISBN: 978-1-944201-01-2

Cover design by Mary Maier
Text design and composition by John Reinhardt Book Design

Printed in Canada

*This Book is dedicated to
Dennis J. Barmore (1950–2008),
whose vision and commitment
made "live" Bid-Whist Tournaments a reality.*

**Special thanks and recognition to these individuals
who have helped to make Whist a great game...**

Nessie Case and Lenora Clinton—CardSharks, Inc.; Directors

George Coffin—Renowned Bridge and card game Author,
American Contract Bridge League Pioneer

Lee and Phyllis Cornute—Founders and Directors
of The Columbus, OH—Whist Players Society (CWPS)

Patricia Cotton, Web Site Designer and Developer

Harold Flowers, Ronnie Ogletree, Tiffany Hutson, et al—
National Bid Whist Association (NBWA)

John Gouveia, Duplicate Whist Director and Organizer, MA

Elsie Jefferson, CardSharks, Inc. Host

Chris Jones (The "Whistmaster"), Author; Co-Founder, NBWA

John McLeod, Multiple Card Games Expert, (www.pagat.com)

Darcy Prather, Author, Bid Whist Software Programmer

Jeremy Rusnak, Founder of Cases' Ladder (Internet Site)

Aaron Haid and **Pat Kevill**, The United States Playing Card
Company, Sponsors of The Grand Prix World Series
of Classic Card Games, 1999–2011

CONTENTS

WHIST: A BRIEF HISTORY

BY GEORGE S. COFFIN
UPDATED BY JOSEPH D ANDREWS

WHIST is one of the original classic card games, predating Bridge, Spades, and Hearts. Its history is interesting and fascinating, and has been featured in a number of books, articles, and short stories. This wonderful pastime has its roots in two card games from the early seventeenth century—the English game of *Ruff and Honors* and the French game of *Trump* (Triomphe). Several card historians have documented a direct connection between Whist and now-obsolete games such as *Hombre, Vint*, and *Ruff*. Edmund Hoyle, (1672–1769) whose name is synonymous with the Rules of all card games (*According to Hoyle*), wrote a pamphlet entitled *A Short Treatise on Whist* in the early 1740s. James Clay, (1804–1873) who was the leading card game authority in the mid 1800s, penned his own *Treatise on Whist* in 1864. This extremely rare booklet is generally considered the first comprehensive work on the game of Whist; it explored bidding systems, and play of the hand.

Whist continued to evolve and was played in the colonies, and for many years thereafter. By the late 1880's, it was the second most popular partnership card game in the United States, eclipsed only by Euchre. Twenty-five years later, the birth of the game of Bridge was to shake the foundations of all Classic Card Games!

From all of these roots and foundations, emerged the contemporary game of Bid Whist. Various modifications over the past few centuries have enlivened the basic forms of many card games, and a few embellishments of genuine merit have persisted permanently. And so, the variations of yesterday becomes the standard of today, and today's new variation may become the standard of tomorrow. Thus, a new game evolved.

For example, in the olden Whist days of our great grandfathers, some chap disliked having to turn his last card as dealer in order to determine trump—only to find it as a singleton in his hand, while holding five, six or more top cards of another suit! To avoid such maddening quirks of chance, this bright person introduced the right of the dealer to state his/her preferred suit. Later, another player conceived of the idea of passing the buck with a 4-3-3-3 (balanced) hand by the dealer's bridging this right to name trump to his/her partner. A few years later (in the early 1900s), a player stuck without a partner in a three-player game proposed the exposed dummy hand. Whist was also played by the Pullman porters on the northeast train routes, and the term *making a Boston* (taking all the tricks in a given hand) became part of the vernacular.

Next came Straight Bid Whist, a competitive one-round auction without mention of suits. Then came Auction Bridge (circa 1905), which featured multiple-round levels of progressive bidding with ranked suits and no-trump options. For nearly two decades, the new concept was tweaked and adjusted. Finally, in 1925, the late Harold S. Vanderbilt, invented Contract Bridge, in which you could not score game unless you had bid it. He also added huge premiums for Slams (six- and seven-level contracts) bid and made. Soon another pioneer, Ely Culberston, added the last major element, *vulnerability,* which helped to offset the advantage of those partners who had already won the first game of a match.

During the Depression years of the early 1930s, the celebrity Bridge matches were front-page news! Then, the great Philadelphia lawyer, Charles Goren, brought Bridge to its zenith with his syndicated columns, TV show, *Point Count Bidding System*, and promotion of the Duplicate concept. The American Contract Bridge League (ACBL) is the governing organization for this game, and is headquartered in Horn Lake, MS.

Whist still maintained its loyal following, Many years passed, and in the late 1930's the original *Straight Whist* (bottom card trump/ no kitty) was replaced by a version with a four-card kitty and one round of bidding. The modern game with a five- or six-card kitty and the use of one or two Jokers was introduced in the late 1940s. This variation became very popular on college campuses, especially in the Midwest and in the South. The two Joker game (Big and Small) with a six-card kitty, soon became the standard. The African-American community promoted Bid Whist in a big way in the 1950s and 60s. Rent parties were a delightful form of entertainment, and often helped to defray some of the living expenses of several families in many cities. Now playing Bid Whist was fun, sociable, inexpensive, and quite competitive!

The continuing growth of Bridge during the 1950s, the post— World War II popularity of Spades, and the South American game of Canasta (popular from late 1940's to the mid 1950's), nearly ended the second comeback of Whist. However, the spirit of Bid Whist's many fans and dedicated players would not let this happen! Thus, a great tradition of card-playing continued for another fifty years and into the new millennium!

The popularity of the Internet, and the development of quality on line programs have been useful as teaching platforms for the new players.

In addition, several Whist books featuring rules, variations, history, and some great stories have been published during the past 25 years.

Live and on-line tournaments have introduced Bid Whist to a whole new generation. Straight and Four Card Kitty Whist are also on the rebound! And the best is yet to come, as more and more people from all walks of life discover a truly great and traditional card game.

This book will feature all three variations, with emphasis on the Kitty with Jokers variation. It contains a number of thematic and illustrative hands.

I encourage you to explore the *Wonderful World of Whist*. You are about to embark on a great adventure!

BASIC ELEMENTS

The Players

The most popular game is *four-handed,* with two sets of partners playing opposite each other. There is a variation in which each person plays individually; however, it is played at special events only. Partnerships may be pre-arranged or determined by the draw of cards, with the two highest, and two lowest cards matched together to form separate "teams."

The Pack

A standard 52-card deck is used. (The two Jokers are added if a six-card kitty variation is played.) There are four equal suits (Spades, Hearts, Diamonds, and Clubs), and the cards of each suit are ranked in one of two ways, depending on what type of bid (and trump/no trump preference):

a. *High/"Uptown" bids:* Ace, King, Queen, Jack, 10, 9, 8, 7, 6, 5, 4, 3, 2
b. *Low/"Downtown" bids:* Ace, 2, 3, 4, 5, 6, 7, 8 9, 10, Jack, Queen, King

Refer to Chapter Two for details on bidding and the use of Jokers. Other variations ("Kitty/without Jokers" and "Straight") will be discussed separately. This section applies to every variation.

The Shuffle and Cut

For the first hand, the dealer is usually determined by having each player draw a card from the pack; whoever selects the *highest* card wins the initial deal.

If one deck is used, the dealer thoroughly shuffles the cards and offers the deck, face down, to the player at his/her right for the cut. The cut should be made toward the middle of the pack. (A cut of less than six cards is not legal) The deck is then prepared for the deal by bringing the two packets together in reverse order. If a card is inadvertently exposed, or the bottom card is seen by any player, the cards must be re-shuffled and cut. Some events require the use of two decks at each table, in order to speed up the shuffling and dealing process.

The Deal

The deal is a basic process in which one card is dealt to each person in a clockwise fashion. The first card goes to the player on the dealer's left, then to the dealer's partner, next to the player on the right, and finally, to the dealer. If playing with a *kitty*, four cards (six cards if Jokers are used) will be dealt to a separate pack. It is always preferable to deal one card at a time and the dealer always receives the last card. It is now a standard requirement that the kitty not consist of the first four or last four cards dealt.

If a card is exposed during the deal, the hand is voided, and must be re-dealt. If there is a "misdeal" (incorrect number of cards dealt to anyone or the kitty), the deal is forfeited, and the dealer must pass to the player on his/her immediate left. After each hand is played, the deal also moves to the player on the left.

Sorting

Players are advised to sort their cards in a logical fashion.. Most prefer to alternate their suits by color. Hands are ranked depending on the preference to bid Uptown or Downtown. If defending, the hand must be resorted. This is an individual preference. Jokers (if used) are always the highest cards in the deck, and should be placed with the suit which is a candidate for trump. Always hold your cards close to your chest. In Bridge, the expression is: "A peek is worth two finesses." Protect your hand!

Tricks (Books)

These two terms are synonymous, although modern players prefer the use of the word "trick." Basically, each trick is a packet containing four cards. (In Joker Whist, the kitty is the first trick, and it has six cards). Cards are played individually, in a *clockwise* rotation, and placed face up on the table. For example, if South leads a card, West plays next, followed by North, and finally East in fourth position. The winner of the trick in play takes that book, and places it face down in front of himself. Each deal (hand) will yield 12 tricks if your are playing with a kitty, or 13 tricks for the original or "straight" game (without a kitty).

Brief Overview

There are three basic phases to every hand of Whist—the *Bidding*, the *Play*, and the *Scoring*. Before we discuss bidding, it is quite necessary to understand the play first. After the deal and the bidding process are completed, the dealer discards the kitty (if playing this variation), and then plays the first card of the hand. This is called the *Opening Lead*. Any card, including a trump, may be led. This first example will establish the pattern for the way each trick is played (this an "Uptown" bid).

In this book, the players are designated by compass directions: North, South, East, and West. Most Bridge columns are written in the same fashion. South is the dealer, and chooses to lead the Jack of hearts. West now follows with his Queen, as North plays the King. East wins with the Ace, and selects a card to lead to the second trick. Note the clockwise rotation.

Suit must always be followed. In the above example, if West had had no hearts, he could have discarded a card of another suit, or used a trump if hearts were not the trump suit.

Here is another example, with a slightly more complicated layout (this is another "Uptown" bid). These are the last three tricks of a hand:

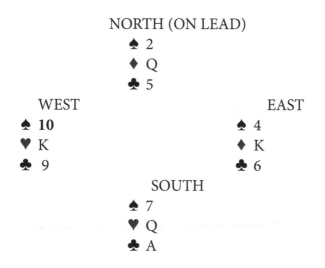

This time, spades are trump. North leads the Queen of diamonds. East covers with his King, and now, South has a choice. He may *discard* the Queen of hearts or Ace of clubs. Please note that if the Ace of clubs is discarded, it does not win the trick, as it is a neutral card. His last option is to *trump* with the seven of spades. The term "trump" describes the *designated suit,* which outranks any cards in the other three suits. In the above hand, the seven of spades is higher than the King of diamonds. Two other synonyms for trumping are *ruffing* and *cutting.*

Continuing with the above hand, let us assume that South chooses to ruff with the spade seven. Now West, who is also void in diamonds, has a decision. He may discard a heart or club, and allow South to win the trick. (Remember, diamonds were led initially.) His other choice is to overtrump with the spade ten, winning the trick. If he does, East's four of spades will become a winner since it's the highest trump card left in the hand.

Trump and trump management decide the outcome of most hands. The only exception is the *no trump* bid, in which the highest card of the suit led wins the trick. In our last example in this chapter, we can look at two possibilities with this "Uptown" hand:

a. Spades are trump.
b. This is a "no trump" hand.

Once again, we are at the end of a hand, and these are the last two tricks:

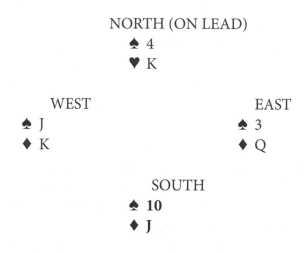

NORTH (ON LEAD)
♠ 4
♥ K

WEST
♠ J
♦ K

EAST
♠ 3
♦ Q

SOUTH
♠ 10
♦ J

Scenario A (Spades are trump):

North selects the four of spades, which is an error. East must play the three, South follows with the ten, and West wins the Jack. West will now win the diamond King, as the Ace has been played, and the trump suit has been exhausted.

Suppose North chooses the lead of the King of hearts instead. This changes the matrix. East may try for a spade ruff (rather than discarding his diamond). South can now overtrump with his ten. West, also void in hearts, takes the spade Jack in order to prevent South from winning the trick. On the next trick, however, North has the last spade, and he wins the diamond King with his lowly trump!

Note that East can also discard his diamond under North's original heart lead, and South will also pitch his diamond, forcing West to use his Master trump (or else the King of hearts will win!). Then South wins the spade ten. It is really amazing how much analysis can be wrung out of this basic two-card position!

Scenario B (No Trump):

North must cash his good King of hearts before exiting with the spade four—which will be won by West's Jack. Each side will thus split the last two tricks. Should North start with the spade four, West will grab both tricks, as the King of diamonds is a winner in its suit.

The lead really decides the outcome of this hand.

After you learn these basics, you will be ready for action!

BIDDING (KITTY WHIST WITH JOKERS)

BID WHIST IS A PARTNERSHIP GAME, similar to Bridge and Spades, which has experienced a revival in America. It is played with a standard 52-card deck plus two Jokers, for a total of 54 cards. In suit contracts, Jokers are additional trump, and always outrank the Aces. The Jokers themselves are also ranked; the higher card is called the *Big Joker*, while the lower card is called the *Little Joker*. (Some decks of cards have two Jokers of different sizes or different colors, to differentiate between Big and Little. If a deck has indistinguishable Jokers, is will be necessary to hand-mark each one)

The object of Kitty Whist with Jokers is to reach a score of +7 points or more, or force the other team to have a score of -7 or fewer. Both teams start each game at zero. The basic elements of the game were reviewed in the previous chapter.

Adapted from "The National Card Sharks, Inc./Official Rules of Bid Whist" (Dennis Barmore) and the Bid Whist page from John McLeod's "Rules of Card Games." Used with permission. For more information on either Web Site, please reference the following:

www.cardsharksinc.com (Dennis Barmore, founder, Copyright 1999)
wwwpagat.com (John McLeod, Editor, Copyright 2000).

Remember that while bidding, you *must* indicate the direction (Uptown or Downtown) if you are bidding a *suit* contract. You do not identify the trump suit until you win the bidding, but you *must* identify it *before* you pick up the kitty. On the other hand, when bidding a no trump, you do not indicate the direction (Uptown or Downtown) until *after* you win the bid—but you must do so before you examine the kitty.

One point is earned for each trick made after the Magic Number (six). Whoever wins the bid declares the trump suit (or direction for a no trump bid) and then picks up the six-card kitty. He/She must now *discard* six cards from his eighteen card holding. If playing no trump, the declarer must discard any Jokers which he/she may have been dealt or obtained from the kitty. Those six cards become the first book for his/her side, as the hand is reduced to twelve cards. The declarer should know just what his/her side needs in order to fulfill their bid.

No trump bids are scored for double points if successful. Defeated or "set" no trump bids result in a deduction of double points. (See Scoring section in Chapter Three)

The Kitty: As mentioned previously, the kitty is picked up by the highest bidder. **The kitty is never "sported" (shown to the opponents or partner).** Refer to section at the end of Chapter Three regarding variations.

PLAY OF THE HAND, SCORING, AND VARIATIONS

Play Of The Hand

After the discard has been completed, the declarer (high bidder) is ready to start. It is assumed that he/she has named a trump if playing in a suit contract, or a direction (Up or Down) if playing in a no trump contract. Now he/she leads the first card. It may be anything, including a trump. Other players now proceed in a clockwise rotation, and must follow, if possible, the suit which is led. If a player does not hold any cards of the suit led, he/she has the option of playing a trump, or discarding a different suit.

A trump always wins over any *side-suit* (non trump) card. If more than one trump is played, then the highest ranking trump wins. Jokers are ranked above the Ace of trump in suit contracts. If there is no trump played, then the highest-ranking card of the suit led wins the trick. The winner of each trick leads the first card of the next trick.

Play continues in this fashion until the last trick has been completed, and then the total number of books taken by each side is determined. The score is logged, and the next deal begins.

Ranking of Cards

As discussed in "Basic Elements," the ranking of cards depends on the type of bid. Here are the rankings from high to low:

1. *Uptown Bids: Big Joker, Little Joker, A, K, Q, J, 10, 9, 8, 7, 6, 5, 4, 3, 2*
2. *Uptown No Trump Bids: A, K, Q, J, 10, 9, 8, 7, 6, 5, 4, 3, 2*
3. *Downtown Bids: Big Joker, Little Joker, A, 2, 3, 4, 5, 6, 7, 8, 9, 10, J, Q, K*
4. *Downtown No Trump Bids: A, 2, 3, 4, 5, 6, 7, 8, 9, 10, J, Q, K*

Jokers have no value in no trump bids, and cannot win a book. The declarer must discard them to the kitty. Any defender holding a Joker in a no trump hand must discard it at the first opportunity (when he/she is void of the suit led) The Joker cannot be used to "stretch" or delay following to any particular suit. (See Variations section later in this chapter.)

Failure to follow suit, when possible, is called "revoking" or "committing a renege." When this occurs, a penalty ruling must be made, and it is usually the loss of three tricks by the offending side. (see Variations section)

At the end of the hand, both sides gather their tricks and determine the results.

Scoring

Each team begins with a score of zero. At the end of each hand, the bidding team will earn points if they make their bid, or lose points if their bid is defeated *(set)*. The game ends when either team achieves a plus score of seven points or more (for a win). The game also ends if either team has a negative seven or more (for a loss). Some groups use the difference between the winning and losing scores as the final result.

At the end of play, the tricks are counted. There are thirteen altogether, corresponding to the twelve cards contributed by each player plus the kitty. In order to score, the bidding team must make their bid. (See chart on page 8) If the bidding team fails to take enough tricks for their bid, they score nothing for the books they did take, and the value of their bid is subtracted from their score. No trump bids have double point values. (Making six no trump would be worth 12 points!) In either case, the opponents of the bidding team do not win or lose any points.

Here is an example: Our team has bid five Uptown, and lost only two tricks. Thus, we made ten tricks plus the kitty. Our side scores a +5. If we bid four no trump and the opponents won four tricks, we would be set and our loss would be -8 points. This would be an automatic defeat if it was the first hand of a match.

Games or matches can end quickly, as one hand often decides the outcome!

Variations

Lots of card games have local and national variations. If you travel to another part of the country, you may encounter a rule or procedure which may be very unfamiliar. The games of Spades, Hearts, and Euchre are classic examples of this phenomenon.

I was absolutely amazed at the number of variations which exist in Bid Whist! The aforementioned Web Sites (cardsharksinc.com and pagat.com) have excellent rules summaries for different variations. Previously published works also feature different interpretations of the deal, bidding, scoring, discarding of the kitty, and other aspects of the game. It is probably a good idea to agree on specific variations (sometimes called *Local* or *House Rules*, as in a casino), before starting a match or organizing an event.

This is the first effort to standardize these variations into some sort of "universal" rules.

Universal Rules

I. Jokers/Wild Cards

    A. *Standard*

        The use of two Jokers (Big and Little) has been in vogue for more than fifty years, and they are the most frequently played wild cards.

    B. *Variations*

        1. One Joker with a five-card kitty.

        2. One Joker and the deuce of spades as a the second highest trump. (In no trump bids, the spade deuce becomes an ordinary spade) – or - Two Jokers and the deuce of spades, thus creating three wild cards and a six-card kitty.

III. Discarding of Jokers (No Trump Hands)

    A. *Standard*

        1. If the declarer (high bidder) holds either or both Jokers, he/she must discard said card(s) to the kitty

        2. If any other player (including the declarer's partner) holds either or both Jokers, he/she may play said Joker(s) when void of the suit lead by declarer. *Or* said Joker(s) may be played at the end of the hand.

    B. *Variations*

        1. A player must exchange any Joker with a card from the kitty.

        2. If a player is allowed to keep a Joker in his/her hand, then he/she has the option of playing it at any time— even if he/she has cards in the suit which is led (often called "stretching" a suit).

These variations affect the play of the hand, and the distribution of suits. If playing for fun, either or both of these could make for a rather interesting game!

III. Bidding
    A. *Standard*
        The full-step bidding, described previously, is the most widely recognized format.
    B. *Variation*
        The alternative ("half-step") bidding process ranks the bidding on the same step as follows:
        a. Uptown (High)
        b. Downtown (Low)
        c. No Trump

Thus, the "half-step" bidding chart would appear as follows:
        a. Three Uptown—Suit Contract
        b. Three Downtown—Suit Contract
        c. Three No Trump

        d. Four Uptown
        e. Four Downtown
        f. Four No Trump

        g. Five Uptown
        h. Five Downtown
        i. Five No Trump

        j. Six Uptown
        k. Six Downtown
        l. Six No Trump

        m. Seven Uptown
        n. Seven Downtown
        o. Seven No Trump

In this system, Downtown bids outrank Uptown bids on the same level. (No trump always outranks any suit bid)

> Thus, it is possible to have this auction (assume South is the dealer): WEST - Five Uptown; NORTH - Five Downtown; EAST - Five No Trump; SOUTH - Six Downtown.

C. *Comment*

Some groups still use "half-step" bidding. Others staunchly believe that Downtown suit bids should not have preference over Uptown suit bids. Most players now favor the "full-step" approach.

IV. The Kitty

A. *Standard*

The kitty is picked up after the final (highest) bid has been declared. It is then examined and any cards deemed appropriate are retained by the declarer. Finally, six unwanted cards are discarded by the declarer. This becomes the first book for his/her side.

B. *Variations*

1. Some groups require that the kitty be "sported" (shown) by the person who won the bid. In other words, the player who won the bid must expose the kitty for all to see before any cards are taken from it. Others require sporting the kitty only when a suit bid is declared.

2. Another "old-timey" rule is the option of picking up the kitty *after* naming a trump or selecting no trump. This is one of the original variations of the game, and is now rarely used.

C. *Comment*

The kitty should **never** be sported. Information can be exchanged by exposing these cards in a certain order. If a player wants to see what is in the kitty, he/she should bid aggressively for that privilege.

V. Scoring

  A. *Standard*

    1. Suit bids are valued at the number of tricks bid. Overtricks are scored as follows: the first two tricks are worth one extra point; then one point for each additional trick. (E.g., a bid of four uptown making four is worth four points; a bid of four Uptown making five is still worth four points; a bid of four Uptown making six is worth five points, etc) In this system, a suit bid can never be worth more than six points regardless of what is bid or the number of overtricks made. Thus, a "Boston" (a bid of seven in a suit contract) is the only way to score seven.

    2. No trump bids are always valued at double the number of the bid. Overtricks are calculated in the same manner. Successful no trumps are usually decisive.

    3. A *Boston* (originally called a "Whist" or "Grand Slam") is worth seven points in any suit bid; fourteen points (and game) in a no trump contract.

    4. A game is over when either team reaches plus seven or minus seven points. Teams do not get points if their opponents are set; the team who is defeated on that hand loses the value of their bid (it is deducted).

    5. Another scoring system is called *Rise and Fly*. **It** is best used in tournaments. Only one hand is played. If the declaring (bidding) team wins their contract, they stay at the table. If the bidding team is set, they depart. No score is kept. Some groups require a minimum bid in order to ensure that one team will be set.

  B. *Variations*

  Game limit is five, nine, or eleven points.

    1. A *fixed* number of hands (three, four, or five) is scheduled (instead of a point limit).

Partial scoring for defeated contracts applies. For example, if a team bids four (suit), and makes eight tricks (instead of the required ten), they lose two points. The game limit is usually set at five points in this variation.

C. *Comment:*

1. The Standard game of seven points is the most widely accepted, although it is distorted by the doubled points of the no trump bid. However, it has stood the test of time.

2. The fixed number of hands approach does have some merit, as it allows a tournament to be conducted without long waits for the completion of some matches. Please note that the bidding strategy is consequently altered, and a team with a losing score will become very aggressive—especially on the last hand.

3. Partial scoring is not sound. If a team is set, they should lose the value of their bid.

D. *Progressive Scoring System ("Whist 21" by Janice Perry)*
Defeated bids are scored as *plus* points for the *opponents*. (E.g., if my team bids five in a suit contract and goes set, the other team earns five points) Negative points are not used. Successful bids also earn plus points. Overtricks are also credited, as described previously. The game limit is 21 points. That may seem like a lot; however, you will be amazed at how quickly a match moves along. There is a premium for defense, as well as accurate bidding.

E. *Comment*
Until this method is tried on a regular basis at tournaments or in league matches, "the jury will still be out."

(Rules may vary for different Whist organizations)

ILLUSTRATIVE HAND

WE HAVE DISCUSSED the basic elements, principles of play, and bidding guidelines. The time has come to review an illustrative hand.

The layout is somewhat similar to that of a Bridge deal seen in a newspaper. A compass direction (North, South, East, or West) is assigned to each player. For the sake of clarity, the dealer/declarer is always the South player, and the West player has the first bid. The "full-step" bidding system is in effect. Two versions of the South hand are displayed. The upper box shows South's hand before the kitty is seen, and the lower box shows the hand after the kitty has been exchanged. The shaded boxes indicate the four hands in play. Jokers are designated as "Big" (B) or "Little" (L). Uptown hands are in descending rank order; Downtown hands are in ascending order. In addition to the hands themselves, you will find information about the type of hand, the final bid, the kitty, and the score. At the bottom is a chart which details the bidding sequence. Most "live" events have their "half" or "full" step bidding systems. Some players prefer the term "Special" when specifying that low cards are ranked higher than high cards.

On the page following the diagram, you'll find a few paragraphs of text describing the deal. Each person tries to make the best available play; however, mistakes do occur in the heat of battle! As you become familiar with the rotation and pattern of play, you will be able to follow the hand with ease.

More illustrative hands can be found in Chapter Fourteen. Most of these hands are instructional, thematic, or fascinating.

Enjoy!

HAND ONE
Theme: "Diligence"

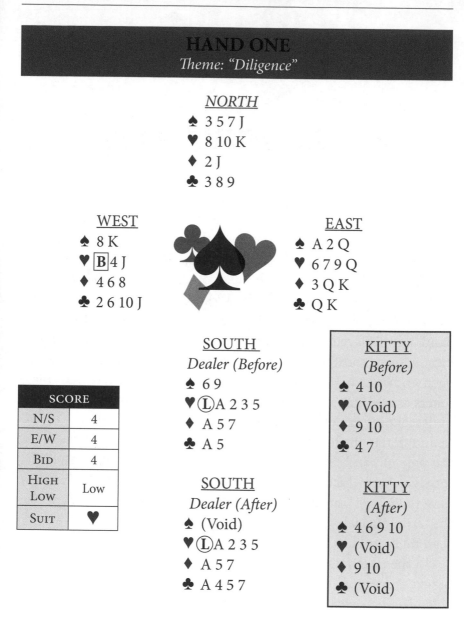

NORTH
- ♠ 3 5 7 J
- ♥ 8 10 K
- ♦ 2 J
- ♣ 3 8 9

WEST
- ♠ 8 K
- ♥ B 4 J
- ♦ 4 6 8
- ♣ 2 6 10 J

EAST
- ♠ A 2 Q
- ♥ 6 7 9 Q
- ♦ 3 Q K
- ♣ Q K

SOUTH
Dealer (Before)
- ♠ 6 9
- ♥ L A 2 3 5
- ♦ A 5 7
- ♣ A 5

KITTY
(Before)
- ♠ 4 10
- ♥ (Void)
- ♦ 9 10
- ♣ 4 7

SOUTH
Dealer (After)
- ♠ (Void)
- ♥ L A 2 3 5
- ♦ A 5 7
- ♣ A 4 5 7

KITTY
(After)
- ♠ 4 6 9 10
- ♥ (Void)
- ♦ 9 10
- ♣ (Void)

SCORE	
N/S	4
E/W	4
BID	4
HIGH LOW	Low
SUIT	♥

BIDDING:	WEST	NORTH	EAST	SOUTH
	Pass	Pass	3 (high)	4♥ (low)

LEGEND: B = Big Joker, L = Little Joker

HAND ONE

South has a wonderful hand loaded with a lot of low card values. His heart suit is very solid, although it somewhat short in length. His partner's pass is a bit discouraging; however, South has chosen to bid four low and selects hearts as trump. If this contract is successful, then North/South will win this game. The kitty is a miserable disappointment with no trumps and minimal help in clubs. After some thought, South deems it necessary to void spades and place faith in clubs as a secondary suit. The ten and nine of diamonds are also quite useless. In Bid Whist, we often take chances (especially if there is a chance to win outright). One does expect to draw something of value from the kitty, or to obtain some help from one's partner. If both of these alternatives fail, a failed bid is the usual result. Sometimes, the only hope is a lucky lie of the cards, or a slip by the opponents. In this hand, a missed opportunity by the West player and a lot of hard work on South's part help to bring home a most difficult bid.

In the game of Bridge, we count *losers* in *suit* contracts, and *winners* in *no trump* contracts. The latter is especially true, as an established card cannot be trumped. The same certainly applies to Whist. Now *this* hand is assessed for losers. The Big Joker is a sure thing for the opposition. There are also two potential diamond and two potential club losers. Since East bid "four high," there is some hope that South's partner *may* have a few key low cards. Accordingly, the Little Joker is led, and West takes his Master trump (North and East discard their highest hearts), and he immediately shifts to the eight of diamonds, avoiding the lead of his broken club suit. North flies with the two of diamonds, which wins. There is nothing more heartwarming than to see your partner provide a trick when the chips are down! (East drops the King, and South releases the seven). North then leads the ten of hearts, as East plays the nine and the Ace wins the trick (West dropped the Jack). The heart two is now cashed, drawing the four, eight, and seven. Finally, the heart three catches East's six, as West releases his King of spades, and North drops the spade Jack.

The club suit is explored, and the Ace of clubs draws the Jack, nine, and King. The seven of clubs is led, and West wins the deuce, as North and East play high cards. The defense now has two tricks, and West trots the eight of spades out. This is covered by North's three and East's deuce, forcing South to use his last trump. The four of clubs draws the ten and partner's three, while the Queen of spades is discarded by East. North, on lead, shifts to the Jack of diamonds as East unloads the Queen and South wins the Ace. The game fulfilling trick is the five of clubs, as the opponent's discards are immaterial. South's last diamond (the five) is cheerfully conceded to the opponents. And the hard-earned four bid comes into the corral after a long chase on the plains! Note that West can defeat the bid by playing the King of spades on trick two (after he wins the Big Joker). This forces South to prematurely ruff East's deuce, and thus, his trump suit is fatally weakened. In Bridge, this play is called *punching*, which is another term for reducing the declarer's trumps. The timing of the hand is now disrupted, as South cannot draw the remaining trump and set up the club suit.

STRATEGY IN BID WHIST

IN ORDER TO BE A SUCCESSFUL WHIST PLAYER, you must be thoroughly familiar with all facets of the game. This includes the "big three"—**bidding**, **play of the hand**, and **defense**. It must be understood that Whist is a partnership game—and we will start right there.

If you have a steady, dependable partner, half of your battle is over. Nothing instills more confidence than knowing that your partner is there for you. There are many times in which he/she will need to provide a key card or make a decisive defensive play in order to salvage a hand or set a bid. The longer you play together, the more familiar you will be with each other's styles and tendencies. The application of Conventions (see Chapter Six) and Card Signaling techniques will strengthen your relationship at the table. If your partner succeeds in his/her bid, a few words of encouragement will go a long way. If your partner makes a mistake, be understanding and sympathetic. After all, you might blunder on the next hand! Repeated displays of bravado, sarcasm, and abusive behavior will result in your playing against a computer or looking for another Whist game. It is a lot more fun to be sociable and gracious, as well as competitive. Remember, we all start out as beginners.

As mentioned before, this is the key part of the game. The game of Bid Whist does have a random luck factor, and it starts with the deal. If your hand is hopelessly full of middle cards, with a balanced distribution, you cannot compete. If you do possess a long and solid suit with a side Ace or void, you have the basis for participating in the auction. Having one or both of the Jokers is an added plus in any suit contract. Other control cards are the Aces and Kings in Uptown contracts, and Aces and deuces in Downtown contracts. No trump hands are based on having several control cards in more than one suit, or a long, solid suit with "stoppers" in the side suits. (Chapter Eleven reviews the Point Count System for the evaluation of hands)

Another factor is the score. If your team is losing badly, or the opponents are threatening to win the game, you may be forced to gamble and bid aggressively. On the other side of the coin, it pays to be slightly conservative if you have a comfortable lead. However, do not be overly eager to sell out too cheaply! Unless your hand is horrendous, be sure that the dealer is forced to take the kitty with at least a four bid. (There is an old adage that the third hand bids high; common sense must still be applied) The standard game is very quick, and one hand can still decide the outcome.

Bidding and the Kitty

The great equalizer is the kitty. In the Jokers variation, it represents 50% of the cards in each hand.

You have won the bid. Unless you have a guaranteed laydown hand ("winners off the top"), you will need help from the kitty and/ or your partner. The time has come to make your discards. The ideal situation in a suit contract is to reduce your hand to two suits. In this way, you will have ruffing or "cutting" power over the other two suits. If you must keep a third suit, a singleton Ace is ideal, or a combination of an Ace and another control card in the same suit is acceptable. Never discard a trump to the kitty!

If you have declared a no trump bid, you will have to decide if you want to cover all four suits, or take a chance by leaving a suit void. Remember, you have the first lead, and that is a big edge. A long and solid suit will "run" all day in no trump hands, as there are no Jokers to worry about! No trump bids have double the points, if successful. The penalty points are also doubled if the bid goes down in flames!

The quality of the kitty is the epitome of the luck factor in Whist, and this is why some players 'bid with reckless abandon. Others are very careful, and will "lay low in the bushes," hoping to spring a "set" on the careless bidder!

The Play Of The Hand

Suit Bids

Everyone who plays this game is taught at a very young age the importance of removing opponents' trump early in suit contracts. The expression is "Get the kids off the street." That is pretty good advice for most hands. After all, you don't want your opponents to be cutting your secondary suit with any stray trumps that you failed to extract. If you have a solid trump suit, and a strong secondary suit, the removal of trump is a very good plan. If your trump suit is shaky, and missing some key cards, you will now have to hope that your partner can help with a trump winner.

It is absolutely essential to *count the trump suit*. There are only fifteen cards to worry about. Experienced players count effortlessly, and can remember specific cards in other suits as well. It is very helpful to note which trump your opponents discard as you run the suit. This will give information as to the location of a key card. Your partner may also give you "count," or show his/her best suit with a high card discard in that suit. Finally, if you have only one trump left, and the opponent has a higher one, it is a much better idea to force him/her to use his/her Master trump on a side suit winner. In this way, you will score your trump separately. After the trump situation is resolved, you can then turn your attention to the rest of your hand, and hope for some help from your partner.

No Trump Bids

You have already made your discards to the kitty. The formula for success is establishing or running a long and strong suit. It is good technique to lead your winning (top) cards in your best suit. Your partner is strongly advised to let you continue playing the hand. If he/she has to take the lead, an immediate return of the same suit is preferred. There are a few exceptions, and one example is finding your partner with a solid suit of his/her own. Occasionally, it will be necessary to force a key card from an opponent's hand. However, if your "strong" suit is full of holes, you may be in trouble. The opponents could gain control and cash their own solid suit—and you would be helpless to prevent this. A lot of no trump bids are speculative, and several are dependent on mistakes by the opponents or finding a key card in your partner's hand. Be sure to keep a wary eye on your opponent's discards. After all, they might be helpful to you as well. Unlike for suit bids, the *timing* of a no trump contract is very critical.

Defense

The game of Bridge has plenty of books solely dedicated to defensive technique. There are at least ten books on the subject of opening leads. Bid Whist is "another breed of cat." Defense has a somewhat reduced role. After all, the high bidder has the opening lead, and the use of the kitty further reduces the defenders' hands to rubble. You may hold one or two really nice suits—only to find that the declarer has voided your suit(s) to the kitty! All is not lost, however.

Defensive partners can really help each other by carefully signaling with informative discards regarding which suits to keep toward the end of a hand. It is good defensive technique to discard your low cards if the bid is Uptown, and your high cards if the bid is Downtown. This can be further refined. The first suit thrown off (usually during the declarer's trump leads) by your partner indicates his/her best suit. In that way, you can guard another suit. A middle or high card discard is an alternative way of showing a strong suit. Another bit of sage advice is to discard a short suit—hoping to obtain a ruff in that suit. One maxim has stood the test of time; "Never lead trump for the enemy."

No trump bids present a different challenge. You can use the signaling system above, or apply some logic and assume that the declarer has discarded your strong suit. Unless you have a sure entry to your hand, there is probably no expectation that you will grab the lead and be able to run this suit. Most experienced defenders will play a "reverse system against no trump bids. The first discard is an undesired suit. The second discard is the pre-ferred suit. This helps to provide your partner with more information. Whatever system you use, be sure that you and partner are on the same wavelength—or there will be "trouble in River City."

Finally, here is a list of standard sequential leads, and count signals. It is effective for no trump bids, and may be used for side suit leads in trump contracts. Defenders and declarers will benefit from this system. The use of Jokers applies only to the trump suit. (A=Ace, K=King, Q=Queen, J=Jack, x=any card lower than a Jack):

Uptown Bids

NOTE: In suit contracts, the Jokers are usually led first, and are removed at the beginning of most hands.

CARDS HELD	SUGGESTED LEAD
A K Q	King
A K J	King
A K x x	King
A Q x	Do not lead from this holding
K Q J	King
K Q x	King
A x x	Do not lead from this holding

x x 2	Do not lead from this holding
Q J 10 x	Queen

Downtown Bids

(SEE ABOVE comment regarding Jokers)

CARDS HELD	SUGGESTED LEAD
A 2 3	Deuce
A 2 4	Deuce
A 2 X X	Deuce
A 3 5	Do not lead from this holding
2 3 4	Deuce
2 3 5	Deuce
A x x	Do not lead from this holding
2 x x	Do not lead from this holding
3 4 5 x	Three

Miscellaneous Advice

Second hand usually plays low (unless a key card is covered) and third hand plays high. For example, if the declarer leads the three of hearts (after he/she has extracted all of the trump) in an Uptown contract, you should play low in second position: This will force his/her partner to play high (in order to prevent your partner from winning with a low card). If your partner leads a low card, you must (in third position) play your highest card (unless the second player has climbed with an Ace or King).

Trust your partner! Always give him/her a chance to win a trick. Never cut your partner's Ace or (high) King in an Uptown suit contract. The same applies to winning cards in Downtown bids. If you are the partner of the declarer, and you obtain the lead, play out your winning cards in order to allow him/her to discard potential losers.

Try to play smoothly and quickly. A hesitation may give away the location of a key card in your hand. And courtesy is always appreciated.

PARTNERSHIP CONVENTIONS

A CONVENTION IS A PARTNERSHIP AGREEMENT, and is a very sophisticated form of "communication." The use of card signals is perfectly legal and within the accepted boundaries of the game. Bridge players are well-versed on conventions, and many signals bear the names of their creators. Jacoby, Stayman, Blackwood, Lightner, and Goren (to mention a few) became household words for devotees of Contract Bridge.

The kindred spirit of partnership card games with a trump suit allows the application of many conventions. Here are my favorite five:

High-Low Signal

This is a very basic signal which applies to suit contracts. Disregard the trump suit, as it will be used for cutting or ruffing purposes. If you hold two, and *only* two cards (from the deuce to the Jack) in any particular suit, you play the *higher* card first (when the suit is led initially).* On the second round of the same suit, you then play the *lower* card which indicates to your partner that you can *trump* that suit on the *next* (third) round.

For example: You hold the nine and seven of clubs. The bid is four Uptown. Hearts are trump. Your partner leads the King, followed by the Ace of clubs. You play the nine first, and then the seven. This

---

* This applies to Uptown suit bids. The reverse applies to Downtown bids.

tells him/her that you will be trumping the third lead of clubs. If you are void of trump, this convention is not used. This signal also works quite nicely if you have the Ace and a small card doubleton in a side suit. The Ace is led, followed by the spot card. Your partner will know you are now void of that suit.

This system must not be used if you hold Ace-Queen, King-Jack, King and any small card, or Queen and any small card of the same suit. The honor cards are too valuable to waste.

NOTE: In Downtown contracts, the face cards are of limited value, as the low cards are premium. However, the signaling concept is the same, albeit reversed. The play of the ten and then the King in the same suit still promises a ruff on the third round.

Low-High

This convention can be used with side suits as well as the trump suit. The lead or discard of a low card, followed by a higher card shows possession of at least three cards in that suit. For example: Uptown bid, you hold 4-5-7 of diamonds. Hearts are trump. If you play the four on the first lead of diamonds, followed by the five (or seven), you are promising at least three diamonds.

Once again, Downtown contracts will require the reverse use of the higher cards as part of the signal.

Lead Sequence

As previously described, the lead of a King promises the Ace or Queen in Uptown hands. The lead of a deuce promises the Ace or the three in Downtown hands. Do not lead from broken suits (e.g., K-J-10 in an Uptown bid or 2-4-6 in a Downtown bid). Connected (natural sequence) leads are much more comfortable, and will convey information to your partner.

TRUMP PETER (ECHO)

In an Uptown bid, the play of a low card in trump followed by a higher card, promises a minimum of three trump. One obvious exception occurs if you have a doubleton and one of the cards is a winner. Some players use a high-low in trump to show an honor card as the third card. It is always best to discuss with your partner which system you are using.

In many hands, the declarer will try to extract trumps as soon as possible. This will limit the use of the Trump Echo.

Discards (Defense)

The *first* discarded card of any side suit (on the declarer's trump leads), signals to your partner that this is the suit in which you have a winning or strong card. This will prevent the both of you from saving the same suit toward the end of a hand. If your partner has led a side suit, and you toss a middle or high card (Uptown bid) or low card (Downtown bid), this indicates that you like this suit.

For example: The bid is Uptown and your partner leads the King of diamonds. You hold the Ace, ten, eight, and three. Drop the ten to show possession of the Ace. Your partner's lead has already promised the Queen. This strategy can be very helpful when defending or declaring contracts.

Final Notes

There are some bidding conventions as well, particularly in the Straight Whist variations. Lower levels often have special meanings. Here are a few which I have encountered:

a. Any opening bid by your partner at the one level implies a balanced hand, no long suit, and at least three tricks in top cards (three Aces; two Aces and two Kings in separate suits and a desire for the team to consider a no trump bid.)

b. Any opening bid by your partner at the two level promises a long suit of five or more cards, and at least three tricks. It implies an unbalanced hand and discourages a no trump bid.

c. Any opening bid of four by your partner implies a powerful hand with one dominating suit, and a side Ace or two. Never overcall your partner's four bid in Straight Whist!

NOTE: Some Kitty Whist players use three-level bids to show "directional" or "one suit" preferences. In the Jokers variation, this can be very effective, as the three bid is rarely allowed to take the kitty.

KITTY WHIST WITH JOKERS BIDDING QUIZ

YOU ARE THE FIRST BIDDER with each of these hands. the game is Bid Whist with Jokers and a six-card kitty. You sit to the left of the dealer. What is your proper bid in first position?

NOTE: **B** = Big Joker, **L** = Little Joker

Hand A
♠ (Void)   ♥ K Q J 7 3   ♦ 6 3   ♣ A Q 8 7   Ⓛ

Hand B
♠ A Q 9   ♥ K 10   ♦ Q J 10 7   ♣ A K 10

Hand C
♠ 5 3   ♥ A Q J 6 3 2   ♦ J   ♣ A 4 3

Hand D
♠ J 5 4 2   ♥ A 8 6 3   ♦ A 10 3 2   ♣ (Void)

Hand E
♠ Q J 8   ♥ K 8 6   ♦ Q 10 7   ♣ J 2   B̄

Hand F
♠ A 9   ♥ Q   ♦ K J 10 7 4 3 2   ♣ 7   Ⓛ

Hand G
♠ A K Q 9   ♥ K Q J   ♦ A K   ♣ A Q J

Hand H
♠ A 10 4   ♥ A J 6   ♦ A 10 7   ♣ A 9 8

Hand I
♠ A 6 5 3   ♥ A Q 7 4 2   ♦ (Void)   ♣ J   B   L

Hand J
♠ 10 7   ♥ 8 7   ♦ A K Q 6   ♣ A K 10   L

Answers to Bid Quiz

Hand A: Five Uptown (Hearts)
EXPLANATION: Bid five high when you have nine high cards in two suits and a side Joker. You will have excellent play for ten tricks. Only a useless kitty and no help from your partner will result in a set.

Key Cards: Ace of hearts, King of clubs, and the Big Joker

Hand B: Four No Trump Uptown
EXPLANATION: Here is a solid hand, loaded with intermediate and high card values, no Jokers, and balanced shape. The kitty will help you to finalize your decision and if your partner holds one of the key cards, you should have no problem with this hand.

Key Cards: King of spades, Ace of hearts, and the Ace and King of diamonds

Hand C: Five Downtown (Hearts)
EXPLANATION: You hold neither Joker, but you have a solid six-card trump suit, a good secondary suit, and a singleton. The odds of drawing a Joker or side Ace from the kitty are reasonable. In addition, a five bid may shut the opponents out from entering the bidding.

Key Cards: Ace of spades, Deuce of clubs, and the Big and Little Jokers

Hand D: Four No Trump Downtown
EXPLANATION: Although your hand has a void, you do have 4-4-4-0 shape and three decent suits. If the kitty is loaded with middle or high cards you will be croaked. Your partner may have a critical card or two.

Key Cards: Ace of spades, Two of hearts, and the four of diamonds

Hand E: Pass!
Explanation: Here is a sad hand with balanced shape and a wasted Joker and nothing else. There are just too many middle cards, no long suit and losers galore. This hand maybe helpful for supporting your partner's bid, but that's about it.

Key Cards: Too many to list!

Hand F: Five Downtown (Diamonds)
EXPLANATION: Anytime you have a solid seven-card suit and a Joker or any eight-card suit, determine the high or low preference and plan on at least a five-level call. This hand also has great side values, the singletons are outstanding features.

Key Cards: Ace of diamonds, Ace of clubs, and the Big Joker

Hand G: Six No Trump Uptown
EXPLANATION: You have tremendous high card strength, no Jokers, and at least two control cards in every suit. The hand is an odds-on favorite to make at least six, unless the kitty is a total bust and your partner has junk. Seven no trump is very greedy; why throw away an almost sure twelve points?

Key Cards: Ace of hearts, and the King of clubs

Hand H: Pass

EXPLANATION: Here is another classic hand, often called "Aces and Spaces." A "directional" bid of three Uptown might be considered. You have only four top tricks, no Jokers, short suits, and lots of middle cards.

Key Cards: Immaterial

Hand I: *Six Downtown (Hearts)*

EXPLANATION: The hearts suit is a monster with the two Jokers. You don't need much help from the kitty and if your partner has one of the key cards the hand is a lock!

Key Cards: Ace of spades, two of spades, and any low heart

Hand J: *Four Uptown (Diamonds)*

EXPLANATION: Despite its minor card strength (diamonds and clubs) this hand is lacking in distributional values. However, there is enough power here to take some action and a decent kitty will certainly help.

Key Cards: Ace of spades, Ace of hearts, Queen of clubs, and the Big Joker

KITTY WHIST WITH JOKERS PLAY-PLAN ANALYSIS

LISTED BELOW are three sets of contracts, a total of six hands. You have won the bid, and have already made your discards to the kitty. Each deal is separate. I have decided to make these hands interesting and challenging, rather than exercises in cashing out "ice-cold" winners in unbeatable contracts. Assume normal (reasonable) suit distributions, and best defense by the opposition. Use the force, Luke! Your skill and patience will maximize your chances for successful results. Describe your play-plan for each hand:

NOTE: **B** = Big Joker **L** = Little Joker

I. Bid of Four No Trump (Uptown)
♠ A K 3	♥ A K	♦ Q J 10 9 6	♣ K Q
♠ K Q J	♥ A K 7 6 5	♦ A Q	♣ A K

II. Bid Of Four (Uptown) Hearts Are Trump
♠ (Void)	♥ A K J 8 6 5	♦ A Q J	♣ A Q	Ⓛ
♠ A K 10	♥ K Q 9 5	♦ (Void)	♣ K Q 2	B̄ Ⓛ

III. Bid Of Four (Downtown) Diamonds Are Trump
♠ A 2	♥ 3 2	♦ A 6 5 3 2	♣ A 7	B̄
♠ (Void)	♥ A 5 3	♦ Q 9 8 7 6 5	♣ A Q	B̄

Answers to Play-Plan Analysis

Hand # 1

Start the diamonds with the Queen. If your partner has either top card, you will make your bid. (If he/she has the Ace and one or two small diamonds, he/she will let your Queen ride for a finesse). The only risk is that the opponents hold **both** high diamonds, and shift to clubs early. The hand is now dead, as clubs will run all day (after the Ace and a small card are played). Hopefully your partner produces a diamond honor. You will then cash the hand out, and gladly concede a low spade in the end.

Hand # 2

Lead the seven of hearts first. (If you play the Ace-King initially, you may drop an honor card from your partner's hand) If you are lucky, your partner will produce the Queen (glorious!) or the Jack (good!). If he/she has only a low card, then you must pray for hearts to break evenly in order to get four tricks in that suit. There is a sure loser in spades, and a possible loser in diamonds—the latter of which may be taken care of via a successful finesse. This hand has some glaring weak spots, and a good defense will set it. Then again, your partner may produce a spade winner, or the diamond King.

Hand # 3

Lead the Little Joker, and force out its big companion! If partner has it, the hand is a lock, as you can concede two minor suit losers after extracting trump. If one of the opponents wins the Big Joker, you must hope for a successful diamond or club finesse. Run the trump (hopefully the Queen will fall), and then lead the Ace and another diamond. You might receive a favorable lead.

Hand # 4

Cash both of the Jokers and see what falls. Now lead a low heart, and hope for a key card from your partner. An alternative line is the lead of the five of hearts on the first round. If he/she has the trump Ace, you are golden, and can lose two clubs. A trump loser will force you to pray for a club honor in your partner's hand. Two trump losers spell instant defeat! Then again, the opponents may lead the club Ace for you.

Hand # 5

Lead the Big Joker, followed by the Ace of trump. After the opponents take the Little Joker, regain the lead (if a club is led, duck it to your partner). Extract the trump and cash the spade winners. Then push the seven of clubs, and hope for some help from your partner. You might promote the spade three for your partner (by clearing the suit before testing the clubs). Yes, this hand is very ticklish.

Hand # 6

Lead the Queen of diamonds and see what your partner has for you. It is obvious that the kitty must have been terrible! Your trump suit is full of holes, and this hand is "in the tank" unless your partner has two of the four missing key cards (Little Joker, two, three, four). The hearts and clubs will have to wait until later.

I hope you did well on the quiz. If so, you are ready for "prime time." If not, do not despair. A little more practice and you will be fine. Remember, your partner is there for you.

THE FINESSE

NOTES: *This chapter will apply primarily to Straight Whist or Kitty Whist without Jokers. Bid Whist with Jokers is structured differently; however, the finesse is still a valuable tool (especially in no trump bids).*

The advice in this chapter applies to Uptown *Bids. For Downtown bids, the order of the cards must be reversed (e.g, K-Q-J becomes 2-3-4).*

A FINESSE is an attempt to win a trick with a lesser card. Suppose you are coming down to the end of a hand, and need two tricks to fulfill your contract or to set the opponents. You hold the Ace and Queen of hearts. Your partner, who has already made his/her bid, leads the eight of hearts, your right-hand opponent plays the nine in normal cadence. What do you do? If you take your Ace, you will lose the Queen to the King no matter which opponent holds the monarch. Your partner probably does not hold the King as he/she already has made his/her bid and would not under-lead that card. Another indication that your partner does not have the King is his/her lead of a heart, which is probably a neutral suit.

Your best chance (50 percent) is to play the Queen. If the left-hand opponent has the King you would have lost it anyway. However, if your right-hand opponent has the King, the Queen will win the trick, and you will score your Ace on the next round of hearts. Although 50 percent is not a guarantee, it is far better than zero percent. Should you hold the same A-Q combination in trump, your likelihood of winning two tricks with a successful finesse is guaranteed.

Finesses come in all types and shapes. The management of the trump suit is often dependent on a successful finesse.

Suppose you hold K x or K x x of a suit. Your side is one trick short of completing a successful bid. A lead from your left-hand opponent is ideal as you will be able to play the King in fourth position or duck if the Ace shows up. If your partner or right-hand opponent leads this suit, and the Ace does not appear, you must play the King. If you play small, your left-hand opponent may win the trick with the Queen; thus, your best chance is to play the King.

Why? Well, if your left-hand opponent has the Ace, your King was dead anyway. If your partner has the Ace, your King is the winner (it is unlikely that your partner held the Ace in this situation as he/she has already made his bid). The key is your right-hand opponent—if he/she holds the Ace, your King wins. If your right-hand opponent leads a small card of this suit, an exception to the "second hand low" adage applies. At this point, you must play the King and hope that your left-hand opponent does not hold the Ace. There are also situations in a close contract where the play of the King will promote the Queen for your partner if he/she happens to hold her. If the Ace and Queen are on your left, your King would be dead anyway unless your left-hand opponent grabbed the Ace earlier in the hand.

We cannot always expect our opponents to do our work for us. There are instances where we will win "free" finesses and these usually occur when the left-hand opponent under-leads his/her honor cards and allows you to score a King or A-Q combination. There is an impulse to grab your top tricks and sometimes this is correct. However, there are many situations in which you will need to manufacture a trick, and a finesse is a convenient way to accomplish this. Here is a table of finessing scenarios and the proper card to play. Assume that a small card has been led, and it is your turn to play.

# of 'Ricks Needed	You Hold These Cards	Lead From Right Hand Opponent	Proper Play (Specific Card) or Partner	Comment
2	A Q x	X	Q	Only if you need two tricks or are trying to set the opponents
2	A Q xx	X	Q	Slightly higher risk with longer holdings
2	AQ xxx	X	A	With a long suit, take the Ace and forget the finesse
1	K x	X	K	Your best chance
1	K xx	X	K	Your best chance
1	K xxx (x)	X	K	It's now or never!
2	A Q 10	X	Q	Correct if only two tricks are needed
3	A Q 10 x	X	10	Your only hope is that K J are on the right—called a llouble" finesse
2	K Q x (x)	X	K	Your best chance
1	K J xx (x)	X	K	Similar to above example
2	K J x (x)	X	J	You must hope A Q are on right
3	A K J (x)	X	J	Desperate Spot!
2	A K J (xx)	X	A	Forget about three tricks!
2	A J 10 (x)	X	J	Standard techniqueue/ "repeating" finesse

Summary Of Finesses

Review the finessing guide table above and commit to memory the basic combinations listed. Please note that in some instances you may have to surrender the lead in order to repeat this maneuver in the same suit at a later interval. The finesse may provide salvation in an otherwise lost situation.

It is essential to consider when to finesse and when not to finesse. Trump suit finesses are very straightforward. The use of Jokers creates some very unusual situations, such as the finesse of the Ace of trump. Long side suits reduce the potential for successful finesses. It is particularly aggravating to take a losing finesse, e.g., with an A-Q combination, and then have your Ace trumped on the next round leaving you with nothing. The objective is to ensure your contract without becoming finesse-happy. Your partner's leads will often have a bearing on a particular finessing situation. Therefore, use the finesse wisely but do not become overly dependent on it. The wreckage of many "over-finessed" hands is littered on the reefs and shoals of the "Island of Whist."

FINAL NOTE: The finesse is a very useful tool in no trump contracts and in variations of Whist without the Jokers.

DUPLICATE WHIST
STRATEGY AND TECHNIQUE

DUPLICATE IS A FORMAT which has been successfully used by the American Contract Bridge League (ACBL) for several years.

The purpose of duplicate is to eliminate the luck of the deal and to compare your skill to other players holding the same cards. In this way, the strength of each partnership can be accurately determined. There are two versions of Duplicate Whist—*individuals* and *partners*. We will be discussing the partnership variation.

Each hand is a separate entity, and unlike a standard game of fixed number of points, Duplicate is structured on a complete round or match of a predetermined number of deals, or hands. A typical tournament usually features 28 or 32 deals. The *director* is the person responsible for the event, and if necessary, for making any rulings. He/She are there to help and guide.

You will be assigned a pair number and direction (North/South or East/West), then you will proceed to your first round table. A round will consist of three or four hands. At the end of the round, East/West moves to the next highest numbered Table while North/South remains stationary.

Play begins with the use of a *duplicate board* which, in effect, is a plastic holder for cards. Each board contains the same complete deal. The deal is separated into four hands, one for each player.

Partners still play as a team and sit opposite from each other. The number, direction, and opening bidder are clearly identified. In

Duplicate Whist, the left-hand opponent of the dealer has the opening bid and the first lead is made by the player to the dealer's immediate right. Each board holds a hand record sheet, which allows the verification of a hand to be accomplished easily. There is also a traveling score which identifies every contract, final score, and number of tricks taken. Although the bidding is still accomplished in one round, the play of the hand is different. Normally, ' the cards in a typical "fresh deal game" are thrown into the middle of the table, and the winner of each trick gathers up the four cards (book) and places them in front of him-/herself.

In Duplicate, the big difference in the routine is the play of the hand. Instead of tossing the cards into the middle of the table, you simply turn up each card in front of you. If your side wins a trick, your card is then turned over vertically. If your side loses a trick your card is turned horizontally. This facilitates the tracking of all tricks when the hand is over and makes it easy to determine the number of tricks taken by each side. The North player is the scorer. The final score for both partnerships is recorded on the traveling score sheet and the hand record sheet is quickly checked to determine that the right cards are returned to each pocket. It is always a good idea to double check the scores before the score sheet is returned to the board. Both forms are then folded and 'carefully placed in the North pocket of the board (on top of the hand).

Accurate bidding and play is rewarded with a good score. If you overbid, you will be hurt by sets and bottom scores. If all pairs bid and make the same score then the board is a "wash," and everyone receives an average score. If your team has the best score for the board, your side earns a "top," which is terrific! Remember, your performance for each hand is compared to the other pairs in the same direction who also played the same hands! Overtricks are always a premium and at the end of the session the scores are then tallied board by board. The method of comparison is called *match pointing*.

Each hand is a separate entity. Thus, a poor result on one hand can be easily offset by a good result on another. There are two winning pairs for each session. North/South and East/West each produce a representative winner for their Direction. This adjusted playoff then pits the two winning partnerships against each other in one final fresh-deal game.

You will like Duplicate as it will allow you to see exactly how well you do against other players. While the luck of the deal is eliminated, you still have to make the most of the cards you are holding. It is the measuring standard for Bridge, and now it can help move Whist into a new era as well! Hopefully, someday, Duplicate Whist clubs will be accessible on a local basis.

NOTE: *Refer to Duplicate Whist chapter near the end of this book...*

WHIST VARIATIONS II

Kitty Bid Whist/No Jokers

THIS WAS THE MOST POPULAR VARIATION of whist until the early 1950s, when it was eclipsed by Bid Whist with Jokers. Basically, all of the rules mentioned in the earlier chapters still apply—with the obvious exception of the use of Jokers.

Everyone is dealt the usual 12 cards, and the highest bidder wins the kitty. Full-step bidding applies, with the bid of no trump outranking Uptown and Downtown bids on the same level. The kitty exchange is only four cards (instead of six). Thus, more of the declarer's hand is left intact than in the typical discarding situation.

Strategy is changed dramatically, and overly aggressive bidding is punished. The trump suit has its normal complement of thirteen cards. Aces and Kings (Uptown bids) and Aces and deuces (Downtown bids) have full value.

However, the use of the kitty still adds "pep" to the game, and the bidding can be lively. Partnership cooperation is necessary for success. Awareness of the score at all times is essential. This is a quality variation, as demonstrated in the illustrative hands in Chapter 12.

Straight (Bid) Whist No Kitty/No Jokers

In Straight Whist, the original game, the bottom card was used to determine trump. Following this came the one round of bidding innovation. The mention of suits was not part of the auction, and the high bidder named trump after the bidding period of each hand was completed. During the formative stages of Contract Bridge, this type of Whist was very popular. It reached a peak in the early 1920s, and declined steadily after that.

Eventually, it was rendered obsolete with the advent of the Kitty and Kitty with Jokers variations. There has been a movement during the past twenty years to revive Straight Whist.

Since there is no kitty, there is no chance for the declarer to improve his/her hand. High level bids are very rare. Minimum bid is a call of one (instead of three). The typical auction consists of one-level or two-level bids, with an occasional higher call here and there. Thus, the game is replete with many partials, and it often requires several deals in order to complete the typical seven point match. Full-step bidding applies. High and low cards have full value based on the type of bid selected. Defense is now at a premium and often one play can decide the outcome of a hand.

Those who are used to playing with kitties and Jokers may find Straight Whist very slow and boring. Others will be very pleased at the natural aspect of the game, conservative bidding, and its very close kinship with Contract Bridge. The illustrative hands will allow the reader to sample the flavor of this most intriguing game.

Three-Handed (Cutthroat) Whist by Stu Patrick

Here is a new twist in the game, which is perfect for those who like individual variations. It is also ideal for the times when you cannot find d fourth player.

A standard pack is used along with two Jokers, thus yielding a total of 54 cards. Players cut for first deal. Sixteen cards are dealt to each person, and six cards are dealt to the kitty. The first bid is made by the player to the left of the dealer. The Standard Full-step bidding system is used. The highest bidder (minimum bid is three) wins the kitty, and he discards six unwanted cards from his hand. A trump (or no trump), as well as direction, are named *before* the kitty is picked up. All of the aforementioned rules apply, especially those which relate to the use of Jokers. Now for the twist!

The other two players become "temporary partners" and team , up to set the contract. Only the declarer's tricks are critical, as the defenders do not care which "team member" takes a particular book. If the declarer is set, he/she scores zero, and each defender wins the value of that bid. A successful contract scores points for the declarer, and zero points for each defender. Game is 11 or 21 points, and any tied scores are played off with one more hand. (A tie after that is considered a victory for both players)

Suffice to say, this is an interesting variation and one worth exploring.

Two-Handed (Honeymoon) Whist

A very enjoyable and casual variation of the game is Two-Handed Whist. One version was described in Chapter Twelve German Whist. This is the American cousin, imported many years ago!

One deck is used, and it is shuffled and cut. A second cut is made to determine trump. The players decide who will begin with the first draw. Then the play alternates. The person drawing from the stock takes the first card from the top of the deck. If he/she wants this card, he/she places it in his/her hand and then rejects the next card in the deck. (It is permissible to look at the rejected card before placing it in the discard pile face down) If the first card is rejected, then the player on turn discards it, and *must* accept the second card (the first card can never be retrieved once it has been discarded).

Now, the other player draws in the same fashion. Then the first player takes his/her turn, and each alternates until the deck' is depleted. The players will now hold thirteen cards apiece, and the stock will have 26 rejected cards.

NOTE: Only two cards per turn are drawn, one at a time, and a player cannot exchange a card which has already been accepted into his/her hand from a previous turn. Jokers are not used and hands are always Uptown unless the players agree otherwise. A trump should always be taken if it is drawn on the first card. Aces and Kings are also preferred. A void suit is a plus, although this is not always easy to accomplish.

After the stock is depleted, the person who started with the first draw leads the first card. The standard rules of Whist now apply. A suit cannot be trumped unless you are void in said suit. The winner of the current trick leads the first card to the next trick. At the end of the hand, there will be a clear winner with a score of 7-6, 8-5, 9-4,10-3,11-2, 12-1—or a Boston! A typical game is the best two out of three, or three out of five hands, etc.

This is a fun and relaxing variation, perfect for those lag times between the rounds of a tournament.

MORE ILLUSTRATIVE AND INSTRUCTIONAL HANDS

HERE ARE THIRTEEN of the most interesting deals you will ever see. These hands represent all three of the most popular variations of the game:

A. Bid Whist with Jokers and a kitty
B. Bid Whist with a kitty, but no Jokers
C. Bid Whist with no Jokers and no kitty (Straight)

Hand Two	"With a Little Luck"
Hand Three	"The Finesse"
Hand Four	"Decisions, Decisions"
Hand Five	"The End Play"
Hand Six	"Desperation!"
Hand Seven	"Shaving"
Hand Eight	"Trouble in River City"
Hand Nine	"Gyrations, Hesitations, and Wiggles"
Hand Ten	"No Guts, No Glory"
Hand Eleven	"The Great Fishing Expedition"
Hand Twelve	"Believe It or Not"
Hand Thirteen	"The Vienna Coup"
Hand Fourteen	"Really, Now?"

HAND TWO
"With a Little Luck"

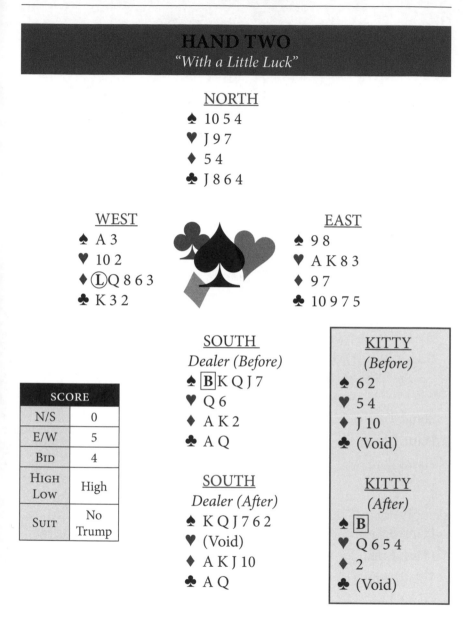

NORTH
- ♠ 10 5 4
- ♥ J 9 7
- ♦ 5 4
- ♣ J 8 6 4

WEST
- ♠ A 3
- ♥ 10 2
- ♦ ⒧ Q 8 6 3
- ♣ K 3 2

EAST
- ♠ 9 8
- ♥ A K 8 3
- ♦ 9 7
- ♣ 10 9 7 5

SOUTH
Dealer (Before)
- ♠ Ⓑ K Q J 7
- ♥ Q 6
- ♦ A K 2
- ♣ A Q

KITTY
(Before)
- ♠ 6 2
- ♥ 5 4
- ♦ J 10
- ♣ (Void)

SOUTH
Dealer (After)
- ♠ K Q J 7 6 2
- ♥ (Void)
- ♦ A K J 10
- ♣ A Q

KITTY
(After)
- ♠ Ⓑ
- ♥ Q 6 5 4
- ♦ 2
- ♣ (Void)

SCORE	
N/S	0
E/W	5
Bid	4
High Low	High
Suit	No Trump

BIDDING:	West	North	East	South
	4 (low)	Pass	Pass	4 NT (high)

LEGEND: Ⓑ = *Big Joker,* ⒧ = *Little Joker*

HAND TWO

"With a Little Luck"

SCORE: E/W +5, N/S 0 • Kitty Whist with Jokers

This is an interesting hand for sure. South has three suits covered, and a partial stopper in hearts with somewhat balanced shape, and opts for four no trump high. (A bid of four high with spades as trump is much safer!) However, there is the chance to win the game outright! The Big Joker is useless in this hand. South examines the kitty after winning the bid, and it does provide some help in diamonds and spades. The heart suit is abandoned, as there is not enough room in the hand to protect four suits. The club Queen is retained as another partial guard in that suit. If the opponents find the weak spot (hearts), they may be able to set the contract—this is the risk that South has taken. *West will be required to discard the Little Joker at first opportunity.* When playing No Trump hands, Jokers are discarded to the Kitty by Declarer before leading to the first trick of the hand.

The Ace of spades has to be removed, and the King is led accordingly. West wins, and contemplates the situation.* His diamonds are long and very weak, and he does not want to underlead his club King. Thus, he stabs in the dark, and tries a neutral suit, hearts. The ten is selected, and this strikes gold, and almost nails the contract! North, noticing the nine in his hand, alertly covers with the Jack, and East wins the King. South discards the diamond ten. The predictable continuation is hearts, and East bangs the Ace on the table, as South lets the Jack of diamonds go. (West and North contribute the two and seven) The eight of hearts is led, as East hopes for the Queen in his partner's hand. South releases the club Queen, and West drops a low diamond, as North comes in with his lowly (and very lucky) ninespot. Any return by his partner will go to all winners in South's hand, as the defense is finished. Four no trump—made!

---

* Unless indicated, small cards are always discarded by the opponents in Uptown hands.

HAND THREE
"The Finesse"

NORTH
- ♠ 9 4 3
- ♥ A 6 4 2
- ♦ J 2
- ♣ 7 3 2

WEST
- ♠ K 6 2
- ♥ K 3
- ♦ K Q 4 3
- ♣ 9 6 4

EAST
- ♠ B 10 7
- ♥ 8 5
- ♦ 10 9 6 5
- ♣ A K J

SOUTH
Dealer (Before)
- ♠ L A Q J 5
- ♥ Q J 9 7
- ♦ A
- ♣ 8 5

KITTY
(Before)
- ♠ 8
- ♥ 10
- ♦ 8 7
- ♣ Q 10

SOUTH
Dealer (After)
- ♠ L A Q J 8 5
- ♥ Q J 10 9 7
- ♦ A
- ♣ (Void)

KITTY
(After)
- ♠ (Void)
- ♥ (Void)
- ♦ 8 7
- ♣ Q 10 8 5

SCORE	
N/S	3
E/W	3
BID	5
HIGH Low	High
SUIT	♠

BIDDING:	WEST	NORTH	EAST	SOUTH
	Pass	4 NT (low)	Pass	5♠ (high)

LEGEND: B = *Big Joker,* L = *Little Joker*

HAND THREE

"The Finesse"

SCORE: Tied +3 to +3 • **Kitty Whist with Jokers**
NOTE: Refer to the Table of Standard Leads

With nine cards in the major suits (spades and hearts), South is very encouraged to hear a bid from his partner. The no trump call implies a balanced hand and possibly one or two Aces. Accordingly, South bids five high. The kitty is another "bomb," however, it does have a trump and a valuable ten of hearts. After discards, for all intents and purposes, he has a two-suited hand. There is one sure loser—the Big Joker—and two prospective losers—the Kings of spades and hearts.

The Little Joker is led, as West and North play low spades and East is in with the big "Kahuna." The Ace of clubs is now played and South immediately ruffs with his small trump. Now the spade Ace is dropped on the table, as everyone follows low, and then the trump Queen is lead. West takes the King and shifts to the King of diamonds. South wins the Ace and tables the heart Queen. West ducks smoothly and North also plays low. When East drops the five, South knows that the King of hearts is located favorably. The Jack of hearts is played, and West is forced to cover with the King. The rest of the hand is now routine as South has all winners. For the record, North knew that the lead of the Queen denied possession of the King (this is a standard lead convention). Thus, it was obvious that his partner was finessing in the heart suit.

Interestingly enough, there is an alternative line of play. South can still finesse the hearts as described before leading trump. North then returns a trump, and South plays the Queen. However, this has a risk factor of allowing either opponent who has a short spade suit without the King the chance to ruff a heart if the suit is breaking 3-1 or 4-0. A much safer line of play is the removal of trump, and the normal play in the heart suit.

HAND FOUR
"Decisions, Decisions"

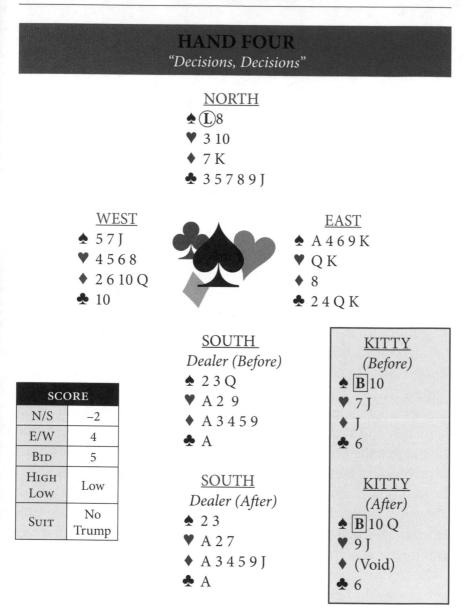

NORTH
- ♠ Ⓛ 8
- ♥ 3 10
- ♦ 7 K
- ♣ 3 5 7 8 9 J

WEST
- ♠ 5 7 J
- ♥ 4 5 6 8
- ♦ 2 6 10 Q
- ♣ 10

EAST
- ♠ A 4 6 9 K
- ♥ Q K
- ♦ 8
- ♣ 2 4 Q K

SOUTH
Dealer (Before)
- ♠ 2 3 Q
- ♥ A 2 9
- ♦ A 3 4 5 9
- ♣ A

KITTY
(Before)
- ♠ B 10
- ♥ 7 J
- ♦ J
- ♣ 6

SOUTH
Dealer (After)
- ♠ 2 3
- ♥ A 2 7
- ♦ A 3 4 5 9 J
- ♣ A

KITTY
(After)
- ♠ B 10 Q
- ♥ 9 J
- ♦ (Void)
- ♣ 6

SCORE	
N/S	−2
E/W	4
Bid	5
High Low	Low
Suit	No Trump

BIDDING:	WEST	NORTH	EAST	SOUTH
	3 (low)	Pass	5 (High)	5 NT (low)

LEGEND: B = *Big Joker,* Ⓛ = Little Joker

HAND FOUR

"Decisions, Decisions"

SCORE: E/W +4, N/S -2 • Kitty Whist with Jokers

The bidding is lively as West opens with three low, North passes and East leaps with a five high bid. South realizes that his hand is limited for defense (surely East will be dumping diamonds into his discard kitty, and his two Aces will not be enough to set the enemy contract). South's low card values and his long diamond suit are encouraging and the low no trump call is warranted. Once again the kitty offers little relief (does our poor beleaguered hero South ever get a good kitty?). The Jack of diamonds does help and the seven of hearts is a marginal card, but that's all there is.

South decides to go for "broke" by blanking (keeping one card in a suit) his Ace of clubs and leaving his spade suit weakly guarded. The Ace of diamonds is led and it predictably draws three high cards. Now the five of diamonds is pushed, as West takes his deuce and North plays the seven and East discards a high heart. If West was playing with mirrors, he would now lead his "stiff" ten of clubs and the hand would fall one trick short, as the club suit is vulnerable. (Here we go with the "hindsight" routine again!) However, the four of hearts is much more logical (and safer); thus, it is selected.

North plays the ten and South wins the Ace. The moment of truth has arrived. Sooner or later South must create a spade trick, and he decides to lead his deuce while he still has a club stopper. West plays the Jack of spades, and North inserts the eight. Now East pauses for thought. He can win the Ace and continue with another suit. South will win any return and the hand will come down to the issue of who holds the heart three. Instead, East ducks the spade deuce with the King and sets a trap with the Ace and four just in case South tries his other low spade. Having grabbed the necessary spade trick, South now cashes his diamonds starting with the low spots, as West follows twice and dumps two low spades. North discards four high clubs. East parts with two high spades and two more clubs.

Finally, South plays the heart suit by carefully leading the seven. His patience is rewarded as his partner produces the one trick that was really needed (the three of hearts), and is alert enough to return a club. North knew that the opponents held the Ace of spades, for his partner would have played it earlier instead of leading the deuce. The Ace of clubs and two of hearts bring home the contract as the three of spades is given up at the end.

HAND FIVE
"The End Play"

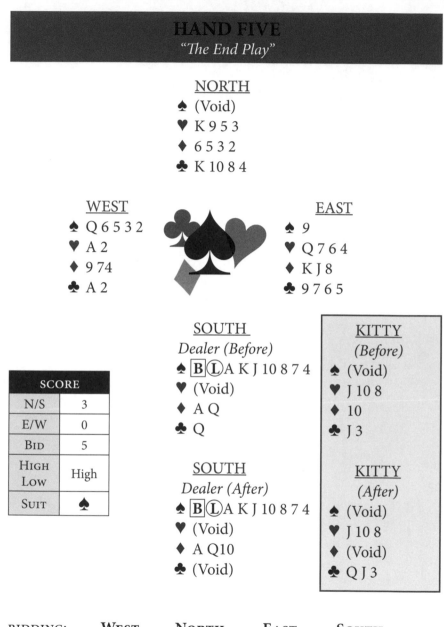

NORTH
- ♠ (Void)
- ♥ K 9 5 3
- ♦ 6 5 3 2
- ♣ K 10 8 4

WEST
- ♠ Q 6 5 3 2
- ♥ A 2
- ♦ 9 7 4
- ♣ A 2

EAST
- ♠ 9
- ♥ Q 7 6 4
- ♦ K J 8
- ♣ 9 7 6 5

SOUTH
Dealer (Before)
- ♠ B L A K J 10 8 7 4
- ♥ (Void)
- ♦ A Q
- ♣ Q

KITTY
(Before)
- ♠ (Void)
- ♥ J 10 8
- ♦ 10
- ♣ J 3

SCORE	
N/S	3
E/W	0
Bid	5
High Low	High
Suit	♠

SOUTH
Dealer (After)
- ♠ B L A K J 10 8 7 4
- ♥ (Void)
- ♦ A Q10
- ♣ (Void)

KITTY
(After)
- ♠ (Void)
- ♥ J 10 8
- ♦ (Void)
- ♣ Q J 3

BIDDING:	WEST	NORTH	EAST	SOUTH
	4 NT (low)	Pass	Pass	5♠ (high)

LEGEND: B = *Big Joker,* L = Little Joker

HAND FIVE

"The End Play"

Score: N/S +5, E/W 0 • Kitty Whist with Jokers

I close this section of illustrative hands devoted to Kitty Whist with Jokers with one of the most beautiful plays you will ever see. This hand was played in a local "live" tournament. It is a wondrous example of card reading and counting.

South is dealt an absolute monster hand, with .both Jokers, and seven solid trump, as well as a side Ace. West's opening no trump bid is passed by North and East, and South reaches for five (high).

His hand looks like a sure thing. The kitty has nothing except the ten of diamonds. Why is the ten worth mentioning? You will see why later — watch this card! The hand is reduced to two suits. It looks like a "lock" for five and if his partner has the King of diamonds, the hand should roll for seven!

The Big Joker is led, as West plays the two, as North ditches a low diamond, and East produces the nine. Noting East's discard, South continues with the Small Joker, and West drops the three of spades as North dumps another small diamond and East pitches a small club. To his total surprise, South now has a trump loser and two possible diamond losers. Rather than test the diamonds now, South opts to put West in with his trump Queen, and hopes (or is it prays) for a diamond return and a free finesse. The Ace and King of spades are played, as West follows low twice and North dumps his last two worthless diamonds. East lets go of two more low clubs. Finally, the Jack of trump is conceded to the Queen, as North tosses a low club, and East unloads his last club.

West tries for a club trick by leading the Ace. North follows with the eight, and East heaves the four of hearts. A disappointed South now trumps with the four. However, South has been taking notes. His partner discarded four low diamonds, an obvious disinterest in the suit. West played the club Ace after he won his trump Queen. Surely, he had to have had the Ace of hearts in order to justify his no trump bid. It is highly likely that he intended a Downtown bid as he was missing two of the top three diamonds (they were in South's hand), and most of the spade tops. The remaining diamond honors might be in West's hand; however, is that the stuff that no trump low bids are made of?

Perhaps some more information may be gleaned by additional trump leads. The spade eight is played and West drops the club two as North releases another low club. East chooses to dump a low heart. The seven of trump nets the diamond four from West (the deuce of hearts would have been better). North heaves the club King, and East tosses still another heart. The last spade is now played and West pitches another diamond, reducing to the Ace-two of hearts and nine of diamonds. North is down to three hearts and East releases his last heart and keeps his diamond suit intact.

The layout is now clear. West cannot hold the diamond King, as would have never pitched two small diamonds leaving the monarch bare or weakly guarded. (He probably does not have the King anyway, as mentioned previously.) North has no diamonds at all. And East has released his clubs and hearts—leaving room for three diamonds. Thus, the distribution and specific placement of the key cards in the diamond suit is determined. Accordingly, the ten is played (yes, that is the same ten which was in the kitty) and West follows with the nine as North lets go of a low heart. East wins the Jack and now places the eight on the table. South confidently finesses the Queen, and is rewarded when she wins. The Ace completes the climb to the top of the mountain. The analysis is so precise here that the alternate play of the Queen of diamonds (instead of the ten) on trick eleven also,works. East will take the King, and be forced to concede to the Ace-ten via the finesse route.

There really is not much more to be said about this hand. East/ West were the victims of a rather extraordinary effort by a gifted player!

HAND SIX
"Desperation"

NORTH
♠ Q 7 4 2
♥ 10 6
♦ 10 5 4
♣ A 8 5

WEST
♠ J 10 9
♥ K 5 3
♦ A 8
♣ Q 10 7 4

EAST
♠ K 5 3
♥ Q 2
♦ 9 7 6 2
♣ K 3 2

SOUTH
Dealer (Before)
♠ A 6
♥ A J 9 7 4
♦ K Q J 3
♣ 9

KITTY
(Before)
♠ 8
♥ 8
♦ (Void)
♣ J 6

SOUTH
Dealer (After)
♠ A 8
♥ A J 9 8 7 4
♦ K Q J 3
♣ (Void)

KITTY
(After)
♠ 6
♥ *(Void)*
♦ *(Void)*
♣ J 9 6

SCORE	
N/S	0
E/W	4
BID	4
HIGH LOW	High
SUIT	♥

BIDDING:	WEST	NORTH	EAST	SOUTH
	Pass	Pass	3 (low)	4♥ (high)

HAND SIX

"Desperation"

SCORE: E/W +4, N/S 0 • Kitty Whist / No Jokers

South is forced to take the kitty as East/West were threatening to win the game. His hand is very iffy; however, the opponents are almost guaranteed to make a three-level contract. East's bid is strategic and South is forced to move to the four plateau. The kitty is terrible with only one trump, thus South is saddled with many potential losers. There are two trump, one spade, and one diamond which are potential lost causes. In addition, another diamond may also be gone if the Ace and ten are long in West's hand. South's partner needs to provide some help. (If his partner had the Ace of diamonds and Queen of hearts, the hand would be on ice for five) This is a classic example of the placement of "key cards" in a hand.

South knows he is in for a lot of work. The hearts are started with the Ace as all follow low, and then the Jack is led. West very smartly plays low (his King is always a winner, and it can wait) and sure enough, East wins the Queen. Reluctant to lead from his Kings, East returns the safe nine of diamonds, and South's King is taken by the Ace. West now makes a very fine play — the lead of the Jack of spades which is covered by the Queen, King, and Ace.

It is now obvious that these opponents are first-rate, and are all over South's case. South can not go after the Master trump (the King of hearts). If he does, West will win and cash the setting trick in spades. The only hope is to find the ten of diamonds in his partner's hand, a somewhat ambitious prospect (let's face it, folks: it is an "off the wall" expectation), but much better than conceding to the spade loser. The ten of spades is marked in the West hand after the lead of the Jack.

Accordingly, the trump King is ignored and the three of diamonds is led. South is rewarded when his partner produces the ten. The Ace of clubs is cashed, as South's spade eight is discarded. His sigh of relief is quite audible! North was the likely holder of this Ace, as neither opponent led it when the opportunity was there. Now another diamond is played. West can win his trump King whenever he wants; however, the contract is assured. South's gamble was very risky and quite necessary. The loss of an extra trick was well worth the price to ensure the success of the hand.

HAND SEVEN
"Shaving"

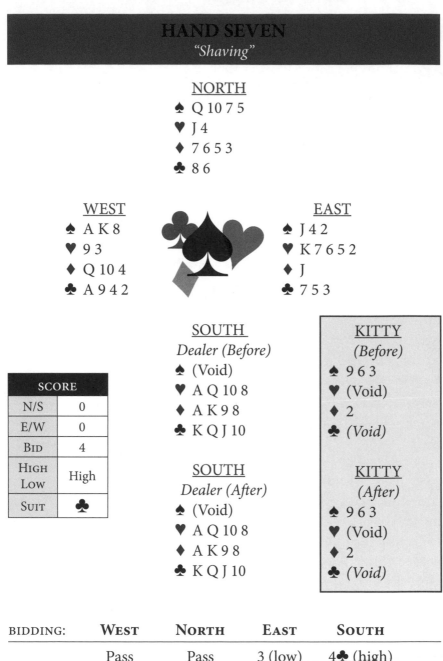

NORTH
♠ Q 10 7 5
♥ J 4
♦ 7 6 5 3
♣ 8 6

WEST
♠ A K 8
♥ 9 3
♦ Q 10 4
♣ A 9 4 2

EAST
♠ J 4 2
♥ K 7 6 5 2
♦ J
♣ 7 5 3

SOUTH
Dealer (Before)
♠ (Void)
♥ A Q 10 8
♦ A K 9 8
♣ K Q J 10

KITTY
(Before)
♠ 9 6 3
♥ (Void)
♦ 2
♣ *(Void)*

SOUTH
Dealer (After)
♠ (Void)
♥ A Q 10 8
♦ A K 9 8
♣ K Q J 10

KITTY
(After)
♠ 9 6 3
♥ (Void)
♦ 2
♣ *(Void)*

SCORE	
N/S	0
E/W	0
BID	4
HIGH LOW	High
SUIT	♣

BIDDING:	WEST	NORTH	EAST	SOUTH
	Pass	Pass	3 (low)	4♣ (high)

HAND SEVEN

"Shaving"

SCORE: Tied 0 to 0 • Kitty Whist / No Jokers

After East bids three low, South selects a bid of four high. He has three solid four card suits and a void. Surely the kitty will be able to provide some support for whichever trump suit is selected. Clubs is chosen because of the four honor cards. Once again another kitty bites the dust as it provides no trumps and three worthless cards in the void suit. (Do you get the impression that several of the kitties in this book are relatively worthless? Not really, but is sure seems that way!)

South decides to keep his hand as-is and dumps the kitty down on the table without any further fanfare. Dejectedly, he starts the clubs with the King, and West pounces with the Ace like a snow leopard! North and East play low and now and West plays the suit that South want to see: spades. The Ace is led, and rather briskly at that. Two small spots appear, and South impulsively trumps with the ten. This is a fatal error. Now he can lead two more high trump but this leaves West with the last club, the spade King, and control of the hand. The hand goes down the drain after West plays his high spade, and South ruffs again. Trump control is utterly lost. If South instead tries to cash his two top diamonds, East will ruff the second round. What a mess!

Can the hand be saved? There is a much better line for South to pursue. After West takes his club Ace and shifts to spades, South must discard a low diamond under the spade Ace and the eight of diamonds under the spade King. Now, if West leads a third round of spades, North's Queen will win (and South will ditch his low heart). North clearly sees South has chosen not to extract trump, and is in need of a heart lead. (If he had any more diamond weaknesses, another one would have been dumped under the spade

Queen) Thus, an alert North will play his higher heart to allow for the finessing situation. If East ducks (playing the King is instant surrender), South will also duck with the ten, and one more heart lead will resolve that suit. (If West had the King of hearts, the hand would collapse) Finally, the clubs are led, and three rounds pick up the suit. South loses only two spades and one high club. North now plays the Jack of hearts for a finesse.

His partner must realize that woodenly leading trump is not always the best line of play. If South wanted to remove trump, he surely would have ruffed either high spade and gone after the trump with dispatch. It is obvious that South is in a lot of distress. In actuality South lost control of the hand right from the "get go," because of his impulse to trump with his winning clubs.

Clubs are now extracted in three rounds, after South wins the heart lead. The nine of hearts drops under the Queen, and the rest of the hand cashes out. But wait a minute — it is not as easy as it seems!

West can foil this by leading a low diamond (instead of a third spade). South is now in with the Ace, and the hand is in deep you know what! If he tries to pull trump, he will lose to the heart King, and the diamond Queen. However, most West players would find it irresistible to continue with spades in order to force South's hand. That is what the game is all about.

There is a lot of analysis here. The theme of this hand is to understand alternative lines of play which provide opportunities to make bids which would otherwise be lost. If the opponents happen to come up with the best defense, all you can do is tip your hat to them and move on to the next deal.

For the record, this hand was played in a tournament and the "post-mortem" and "as it turns out" analysis continued for more than twenty minutes!

HAND EIGHT
"Trouble in River City"

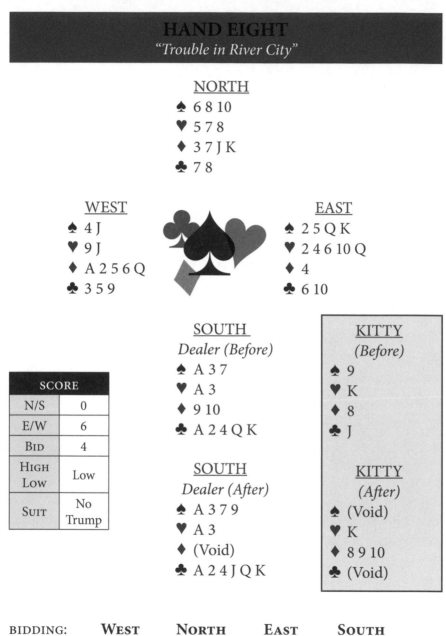

NORTH
♠ 6 8 10
♥ 5 7 8
♦ 3 7 J K
♣ 7 8

WEST
♠ 4 J
♥ 9 J
♦ A 2 5 6 Q
♣ 3 5 9

EAST
♠ 2 5 Q K
♥ 2 4 6 10 Q
♦ 4
♣ 6 10

SOUTH
Dealer (Before)
♠ A 3 7
♥ A 3
♦ 9 10
♣ A 2 4 Q K

KITTY
(Before)
♠ 9
♥ K
♦ 8
♣ J

SCORE	
N/S	0
E/W	6
Bid	4
High Low	Low
Suit	No Trump

SOUTH
Dealer (After)
♠ A 3 7 9
♥ A 3
♦ (Void)
♣ A 2 4 J Q K

KITTY
(After)
♠ (Void)
♥ K
♦ 8 9 10
♣ (Void)

BIDDING:	WEST	NORTH	EAST	SOUTH
	3 (low)	Pass	4 (low)	4 NT (low)

HAND EIGHT

"Trouble in River City"

SCORE: E/W +6, N/S 0 • Kitty Whist / No Jokers

North/South are in desperate straits, losing by a score of six to zero. East bids four low in order to force South to the five-level, however, South opts for four no trump. He just cannot resist the lure of eight points and instant victory! Thus we have the peculiarity of two consecutive Downtown bids. The kitty provides only one helpful card. The diamond suit is abandoned and a very risky contract is in place.

South starts the clubs with the Ace, and then the deuce as West tosses the nine and five, and North and East release their middle spot cards. The King of clubs is conceded to West's three, North drops the spade ten, and East drops the King of Spades. West immediately shifts to the diamond Ace. South is now praying tlit his partner has a diamond stopper — otherwise it is lights out! North unloads his King of diamonds and East plays the four, as South dumps the spade nine. The diamond two is continued and it finds North's Jack, East's. Queen of hearts, and South's seven of spades. West's six of diamonds is taken by North's three as East unloads the ten of hearts and South heaves the spade *three*. South has discarded three spades on the previous diamond plays—thus, he has no real interest in this suit. Therefore, North applies a bit of logic, and shifts to a high heart. East smoothly plays the six (rather than sacrifice his deuce), and South is put to the test. Without hesitation, the three of hearts is finessed, and it wins. This is a sure thing, as the East player had made a downtown bid, and was marked with the major suit deuces. The hand is now cashed out for a successful conclusion.

A fascinating aspect of this hand is that South can discard the *three of hearts* on the third round of diamonds. Will North be alert to lead a *spade* after he wins his diamond? The same finessing position applies! Surely, South's ditching of three consecutive spades was much more of message to his partner to select the other major suit for the critical return. (South would not have discarded the spade three if he held the deuce of that suit; thus he must have reduced to the spade Ace and needed a heart return) This is another example of partnership cooperation and card-reading at the highest level.

HAND NINE
"Gyrations, Hesitations, and Wiggles"

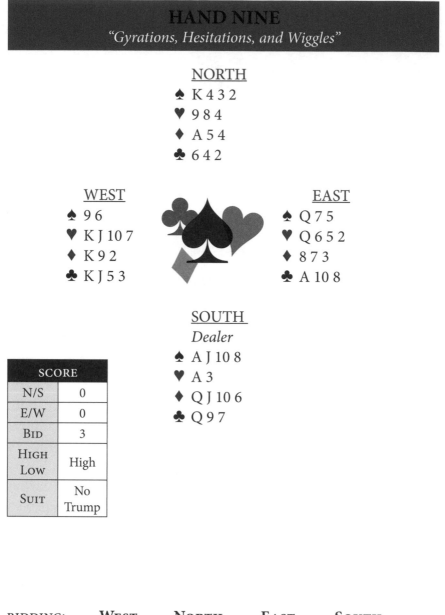

NORTH
- ♠ K 4 3 2
- ♥ 9 8 4
- ♦ A 5 4
- ♣ 6 4 2

WEST
- ♠ 9 6
- ♥ K J 10 7
- ♦ K 9 2
- ♣ K J 5 3

EAST
- ♠ Q 7 5
- ♥ Q 6 5 2
- ♦ 8 7 3
- ♣ A 10 8

SOUTH
Dealer
- ♠ A J 10 8
- ♥ A 3
- ♦ Q J 10 6
- ♣ Q 9 7

SCORE	
N/S	0
E/W	0
Bid	3
High Low	High
Suit	No Trump

BIDDING:	WEST	NORTH	EAST	SOUTH
	Pass	3 (low)	Pass	3 NT (high)

HAND NINE

"Gyrations, Hesitations, and Wiggles"

SCORE: 0 to 0 • Straight Whist / No Kitty

West passes and North opens with three low. South, after much thought, decides to bid three no trump high. This is a.very ambitious undertaking and truly in need of some great breaks. However, it is a new game!

The Queen of diamonds is opened, and West flinches slightly, as he gawks at his King and decides to play low. North alertly ducks with his four (the lead of the Queen denies the King) and East plays the three, thereby justifying West's "hitch." South repeats the finesse with the Jack and this time, West plays a predictable King (lucky break number one). North takes the Ace and dutifully returns the five. The ten wins as West follows and a happy South realizes the suit is breaking evenly (lucky break number two). The lowly six of diamonds is cashed and all the other players toss low hearts.

Now the Jack of spades is led (this denies possession of the Queen—these lead conventions are sure helpful), and with light ening speed, West dumps the six. This 'indicates a great indifference to the suit-led. North grabs the King and returns the four of spades; East funibles slightly and produces the seven and South now finesses the ten. West's discard of the nine confirms the likely layout of the suit (lucky break number three). The Ace of spades is played as West dumps a low club and a gleeful South observes the drop of the Queen. East mutters that he should have held his cards closer to his chest and comments that a peek is worth two finesses. The Ace of hearts and the last spade reel in another successful contract. Three no trump is made with four spades, four diamonds, and one heart. The club suit is immaterial, and the last four tricks are given up.

This is a wonderful example of reading cards and body language.

HAND TEN
"No Guts, No Glory"

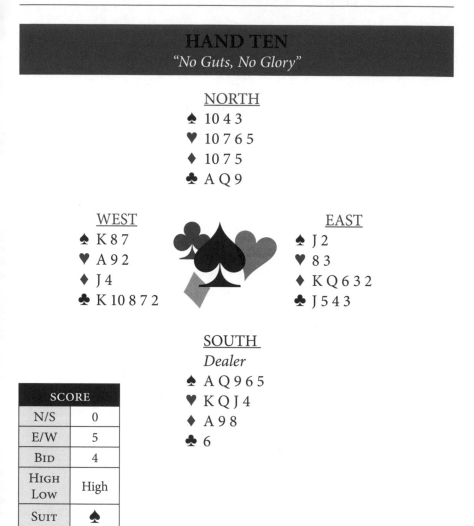

NORTH
- ♠ 10 4 3
- ♥ 10 7 6 5
- ♦ 10 7 5
- ♣ A Q 9

WEST
- ♠ K 8 7
- ♥ A 9 2
- ♦ J 4
- ♣ K 10 8 7 2

EAST
- ♠ J 2
- ♥ 8 3
- ♦ K Q 6 3 2
- ♣ J 5 4 3

SOUTH
Dealer
- ♠ A Q 9 6 5
- ♥ K Q J 4
- ♦ A 9 8
- ♣ 6

SCORE	
N/S	0
E/W	5
Bid	4
High Low	High
Suit	♠

BIDDING:	WEST	NORTH	EAST	SOUTH
	Pass	Pass	3 (low)	4♠ (high)

HAND TEN

"No Guts No Glory"

SCORE: Tied +4 to +4 • Straight Whist / No Kitty

West and North pass and East bids three low. South with nine cards in the major suits, a side Ace, and a singleton, decides to overcall with four high and selects spades as trump. The hand has some "turbulence" and he will need a little help from his partner.

Because West passed and East bid low, there are some logical expectations for North to hold at least one or two winners. The six of clubs is led, as South plans to ruff this suit with his low trump. There is also the chance that his partner may have a winner or two in this suit. West plays the two and North finesses the Queen, as East drops the three. North did take a chance; however, East's low bid probably denied possession of the King. (An ambitious expectation !) The Ace of clubs is cashed and South is thrilled to unload the diamond eight. Eschewing the club suit, North decides to play on trump and leads the ten. East covers with the Jack and South plays the Queen, as West wins the King. (Had East played low under the ten of spades, South admitted that he would have also played low—an unusual double finesse).

The Ace of hearts is won by West and everyone plays small. A small heart is taken by South's King. The Ace of spades is played, followed by the nine as the trump suit is resolved. A diamond is cheerfully conceded at the end of the hand and the four bid is brought home. Once again, a daring play by a partner has saved the bacon!

This hand is a prime example of depending on the finesse.

"Sometimes you get the bear, and sometimes the bear gets you"!

HAND ELEVEN
"The Great Fishing Expedition"

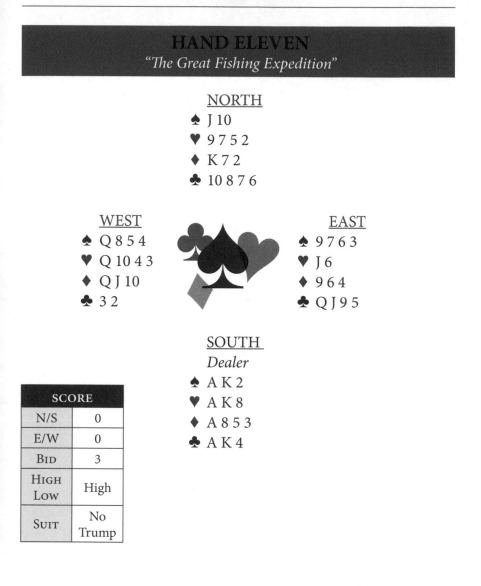

NORTH
- ♠ J 10
- ♥ 9 7 5 2
- ♦ K 7 2
- ♣ 10 8 7 6

WEST
- ♠ Q 8 5 4
- ♥ Q 10 4 3
- ♦ Q J 10
- ♣ 3 2

EAST
- ♠ 9 7 6 3
- ♥ J 6
- ♦ 9 6 4
- ♣ Q J 9 5

SOUTH
Dealer
- ♠ A K 2
- ♥ A K 8
- ♦ A 8 5 3
- ♣ A K 4

SCORE	
N/S	0
E/W	0
Bid	3
High Low	High
Suit	No Trump

BIDDING:	WEST	NORTH	EAST	SOUTH
	Pass	Pass	Pass	3 NT (high)

HAND ELEVEN

"The Great Fishing Expedition"

Score: Tied 0 to 0 • Straight Whist /No Kitty

South has seven top tricks and ops for an ambitious three no trump high. His hand is loaded with prime values; however, there is no long running suit and no intermediate cards. Hopefully, his partner will have some support. This seems to be a recurring theme; however, if Whist was an individual's game, there would be need no for this or any other book about the game! Thus, we must depend on a reliable and alert partner, who can come through with the right plays. Meanwhile, back to the hand!

Another alternative is to establish a winning diamond. This is a rather big order. The three of diamonds is led and West's Queen is covered by North's King. Now the eighth trick is in the bag. North shifts to the spade Jack, as he decides that his two weak honor cards may be helpful to his partner (it is usually a good idea to return your partner's led suit). In this way, if your partner's led suit fails, you will not be criticized. There are those times, however, when creative reasoning is worthy of consideration. East drops the three under the Jack and South plays the two as he tries for the finesse. West is in with the Queen and leads the three of hearts. North ducks and East's Jack is taken by the King. The Ace of diamonds is quickly cashed as everyone follows low, and then another diamond is won by West's Jack. For the third time in this book, a diamond suit has broken evenly. It is quite obvious that this is a great year for diamonds. (Last year was wonderful for hearts) Nine tricks are now assured, and that's just enough for the city.

HAND TWELVE
"Believe It or Not"

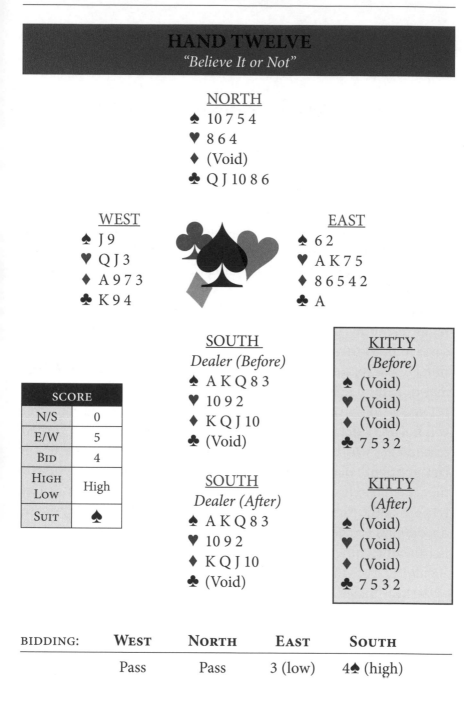

NORTH
- ♠ 10 7 5 4
- ♥ 8 6 4
- ♦ (Void)
- ♣ Q J 10 8 6

WEST
- ♠ J 9
- ♥ Q J 3
- ♦ A 9 7 3
- ♣ K 9 4

EAST
- ♠ 6 2
- ♥ A K 7 5
- ♦ 8 6 5 4 2
- ♣ A

SOUTH
Dealer (Before)
- ♠ A K Q 8 3
- ♥ 10 9 2
- ♦ K Q J 10
- ♣ (Void)

KITTY
(Before)
- ♠ (Void)
- ♥ (Void)
- ♦ (Void)
- ♣ 7 5 3 2

SOUTH
Dealer (After)
- ♠ A K Q 8 3
- ♥ 10 9 2
- ♦ K Q J 10
- ♣ (Void)

KITTY
(After)
- ♠ (Void)
- ♥ (Void)
- ♦ (Void)
- ♣ 7 5 3 2

SCORE	
N/S	0
E/W	5
BID	4
HIGH LOW	High
SUIT	♠

BIDDING:	WEST	NORTH	EAST	SOUTH
	Pass	Pass	3 (low)	4♠ (high)

HAND TWELVE

"Believe It or Not"

SCORE: E/W +5, N/S +3 • Kitty Whist / No Jokers

Here is a deal which is "magical." David Copperfield would be very impressed by the way the losers in South's hand disappear! Perhaps the hand really is quicker than the eye!

Two passes, and a three low bid come to South, and he lurches at four high—reaching for game. He does have a void and two strong suits. The kitty yields four small clubs, and it is rejected in a flash! The hand has the appearance of four losers—one high diamond and three hearts. Perhaps his partner has a winner in the diamond or heart suit.

The diamond King is led and West plays the Ace as he mutters to himself, "always cover an honor with an honor." He does proclaim that Aces were meant to take Kings, but is shocked when North trumps with the four. North, who understands that his trump may be needed for more diamond ruffs, rejects the automatic return of a spade, and selects a low club, instead. East produces the Ace and South trumps the with the three as West tosses the four. Three high diamonds, one at a time, are led by South as East and West helplessly follow and North dumps his entire heart suit! The ten of hearts is dropped on the table, and West plays his Queen. North trumps with the five (East plays the five), and returns the Jack of clubs. East discards a low diamond and South ruffs with the eight as West drops the nine of clubs.

The heart nine is ducked with the three. North ruffs with his seven, and East, with much disgust, pitches the seven. Another club by North is ruffed by East's six, as he vainly tries to disrupt the hand. South produces the spade Queen, as West's King falls. South's last heart is ruffed with the ten, and East drops the King. The last two tricks are taken by the Ace and King of spades, and the hand makes seven!

Amazing, eh? Believe it or not!

HAND THIRTEEN
"The Vienna Coup"

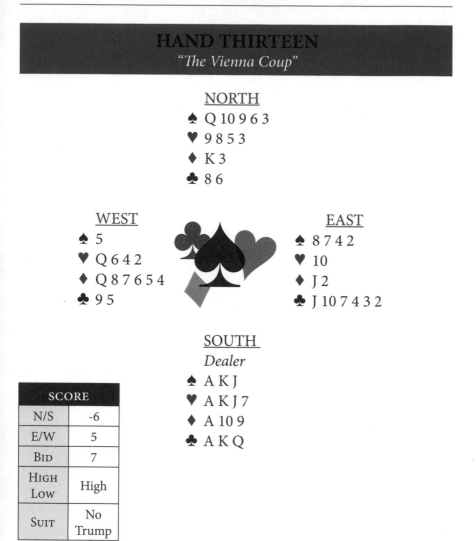

NORTH
- ♠ Q 10 9 6 3
- ♥ 9 8 5 3
- ♦ K 3
- ♣ 8 6

WEST
- ♠ 5
- ♥ Q 6 4 2
- ♦ Q 8 7 6 5 4
- ♣ 9 5

EAST
- ♠ 8 7 4 2
- ♥ 10
- ♦ J 2
- ♣ J 10 7 4 3 2

SOUTH
Dealer
- ♠ A K J
- ♥ A K J 7
- ♦ A 10 9
- ♣ A K Q

SCORE	
N/S	-6
E/W	5
Bid	7
High Low	High
Suit	No Trump

BIDDING:	WEST	NORTH	EAST	SOUTH
	Pass	Pass	4 (low)	7 NT (high)

HAND THIRTEEN
"The Vienna Coup"

SCORE: E/W +5, N/S -6 • **Straight Whist / No Kitty**

Next, we offer an example of the one of the prettiest and rarest plays in Whist. James Clay, a leading authority on the game more than 100 years ago, first published the Vienna Coup as a problem-solving hand in a booklet entitled "Treatise on Whist" (1864).

The bidding has proceeded with two passes and a three low bid by East. South, in need of lots of points, examines his hand. There are eight top tricks with the opportunity for a few more via favorable card location. Already in arrears by eleven points, and at the limit, the time has come to "go for the gold." Thus, a seven no trump bid is declared, with high cards as winners. This is as wild a bid as you will ever see! *A safe and simple bid of "4 High" would have sufficed!*

The first order of business is the club suit, and it is cashed right off the top. The hope is to set up a trick or two in partner's hand, and then to find an entry. Everyone follows low on the first two leads, and the Queen of clubs draws a low diamond discard by West and the heart three from North. East's four reveals the massive stack of the remaining clubs in his hand. The nine of diamonds is lead, West plays the five, and North's King fetches the deuce. A low spade by North now draws another deuce by East, as South wins with his Ace. The King of spades is cashed as West tosses another low diamond, and North and East play the six and four respectively.

South pauses for thought. Perhaps the Queen of hearts is doubleton; if that is the case, then the Jack will be good for another trick. His partner has shown an interest in spades by leading that suit after winning the first diamond trick. Thus, the Ace and King of hearts are cashed as West plays two small spots, North lets go of the five and eight, and East releases the heart ten (which catches North's eye) and club seven. The Queen of hearts is now a winner in West's hand.

Little does South know that he is playing one of the most beautiful and classic squeezes which is rarely executed!

The Jack of spades catches the six of hearts from West. North overtakes with his Queen, and East dumps the seven. The spade ten draws East's last spot, as South ditches the heart seven, and West plays the diamond seven. We are now down to this position:.

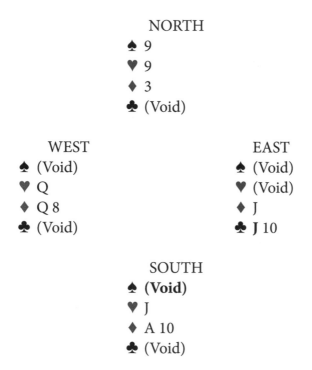

NORTH
♠ 9
♥ 9
♦ 3
♣ (Void)

WEST
♠ (Void)
♥ Q
♦ Q 8
♣ (Void)

EAST
♠ (Void)
♥ (Void)
♦ J
♣ J 10

SOUTH
♠ **(Void)**
♥ J
♦ A 10
♣ (Void)

North leads the spade nine and East plays his club ten. South now pitches the Jack of hearts, and West is squeezed to the limit. If he throws his small diamond, then South's Ace and ten are winners. (North will simply lead the diamond three, and scoop East's Jack and the now bare Queen!) If West lets go of the heart Queen, then North's nine is a winner. (He will take the heart nine and South will then toss his low diamond, and the Ace will win the last trick) It just does not get any better than this! Seven no trump bid and made! Game, Set, and Match!

HAND FOURTEEN
"Really, Now?"

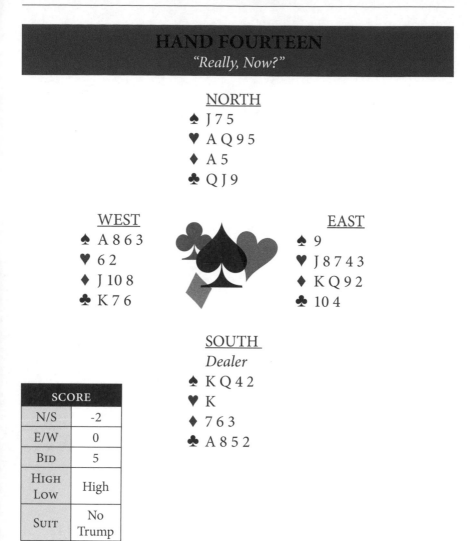

NORTH
♠ J 7 5
♥ A Q 9 5
♦ A 5
♣ Q J 9

WEST
♠ A 8 6 3
♥ 6 2
♦ J 10 8
♣ K 7 6

EAST
♠ 9
♥ J 8 7 4 3
♦ K Q 9 2
♣ 10 4

SOUTH
Dealer
♠ K Q 4 2
♥ K
♦ 7 6 3
♣ A 8 5 2

SCORE	
N/S	-2
E/W	0
BID	5
HIGH LOW	High
SUIT	No Trump

BIDDING:

WEST	NORTH	EAST	SOUTH
Pass	Pass	Pass	5 NT (high)

"The Kitty has already been discarded"

(♠ 10, ♥ 10, ♦ 4, ♣ 3)

HAND FOURTEEN

"Really, Now?"

Score: E/W 0, N/S -2 • Kitty Whist / No Jokers

This hand appeared in a recent tournament that featured this version of Whist. One of my friends transcribed this hand and sent it to me. He asked that the play be analyzed. The crux of the issue was the soundness of the five no trump bid. The kitty had already been discarded (I wonder why the spade ten was dumped). Remember, this was a live event.

South was on lead and immediately led his lonely King of hearts. I surmise that this was some sort of "unblocking" play. Next came the spade two, and West grabbed the Ace with the speed of light! The Jack of diamonds was a great shift, and North took the Ace as East dropped a very emphatic King. This was a loud signal to his partner to return diamonds if and when he had the lead again. The club Queen was played by North and when East played low, South also ducked (correctly). West won the King and, for some interesting reason, chose the six of hearts for his next lead!

According to the account, the East player rolled his eyes back, let out a groan of disgust, and muttered something about "sun on the beach!" He then proclaimed to his partner, "You have two excuses for not returning a diamond—you are void of the suit, or you are having a heart attack." West shrunk back in his chair as North won the Ace of hearts and East dropped the four. South heaved his diamond six. The heart Queen was cashed, followed by the seven. South tossed the four of spades (a terrible blunder) and West dumped a low club. North, still on lead, pushed the Jack of clubs, which fetched the ten, five, and seven.

South's errant discard of the low spade doomed his side to defeat. No matter what his partner now played, the hand was lost.

North finally selected the club nine and, after thrashing around, South displayed the white flag. The seven of diamonds was conceded to the opponents. West was greatly relieved to get rid of the "goat horns." My final comment about South's play: not all butchers work in a meat shop!

GLOSSARY OF TERMS

AUCTION: The interval during which the bidding occurs.

BALANCED HAND: A hand which has a "symmetrical shape," with no voids, singletons, or long suits. This usually applies to hands that are 4 – 4 – 3 – 2 or 4 – 3 – 3 – 3.

BID: A number (from one to seven) indicating a contract level

BIG: The term for the Large Joker, the highest ranking trump in the deck.

BLANKING: Voiding yourself of a suit. (Some experts also use this term for reducing a suit to a singleton honor card)

BLOCKED: Describes a suit in which there is no transportation or communication between both partners' hands.

BOARDED: Indicates the play of a card which has been exposed and touched the table.

BOOK: A packet of four cards; synonymous with "trick." (There are 13 tricks in the typical whist hand) Also used to describe the minimum of six tricks a side must take before it can earn points.

BONUS (SCORING): Points awarded for overtricks. The first two tricks in excess of the bid yield an extra point; additional tricks yield one point each. (A bid of four making seven is worth six points)

"BOSTON": When a partnership takes all 13 tricks in a hand. (The equivalent of the "Grand Slam" in Bridge This term was "coined" by the Pullman Porters during the glory days of the railroads.

BREAK: The distribution of a suit between both partnerships. Also used to describe the luck of a particular suit layout.

BROKEN: Jargon for the playing of a trump for the first time. **Also a term for a suit which has non connected high cards (A – Q – 10; K – J – 9; K – 10 – 8, etc.)**

CALL: Another word for "bid."

CASH: To play established winning card(s) of any suit.

CHEATING: A deliberate attempt by a player or partnership to circumvent the rules of the game. Examples include: use of "body language," peeking at another player's hand, incorrectly recording the score, or talking in a manner to convey information about one's hand.

CLAIM: An announcement by a particular player indicating that the balance of tricks are guaranteed by his/her side. Akin to "laydown," but different in that a "claim is made toward the end of a hand.

CONTRACT: The highest bid at the conclusion of the auction specifying the level and type of bid. (E.g., a bid of four no trump calls for ten tricks, and no designated trump suit)

CONTROL: A key high card, or a "stopper" in a suit.

CONVENTION: A partnership agreement denoting a specific meaning to a play or discard.

COVER: To play a higher card of the suit led, and usually applicable to "face cards" in Uptown bids. May also be the play of lower cards of the suit led in Downtown bids.

CROSS-RUFF: Separate or alternate trumping of respective side suits by the members of the same partnership.

CUT: Trumping or ruffing. Also applies to dividing a deck into two packs prior to the deal.

DEAL: The distributing of the cards in a clockwise rotation to each of the players. Also the collective term for all of the cards dealt in every hand.

DECLARER: The person who has the high bid, and names trump (or no trump). This term is taken from the game of Bridge.

DEFENDER (DEFENSE): The term for the partnership which attempts to set or defeat their opponent's bid.

DEUCE: The two of a suit.

DIRECTIONAL: A bid which provides information, such as scattered high card strength, or a preference for a high or low contract. It is intended to support your partner's hand.

DISCARD: The play of another suit, instead of trumping, when void of the suit led (same as "sluffing"). Also a term describing the exchange of cards from the declarer's hand to the kitty.

DISTRIBUTION: The overall shape of a hand, or the division of each suit among the four players.

DOWN: Another term for a "set" bid or a defeated contract.

DOWNTOWN: A suit/trump contract in which low cards win. Each suit is ranked in reverse (A, 2, 3, 4, etc). Jokers (when used) are always ranked as the winning trump in suit contracts.— "Special" is another term for "Downtown".

DOUBLETON: Holding exactly two cards in any given suit.

DRAW: Another word for exhausting or extracting the opponent's trump suit.

DUCK: A strategic play of a low card usually intended to allow your partner the chance to win the trick.

DUPLICATE: A variation of Bridge or Whist in which all of the competitors play the same hands. Results are then compared for the best scores. The hands are contained in special holders ("boards"). The luck of the deal is all but eliminated.

DUPLICATION: Equal values in the same suit distributed between a partnership. (E.g., you hold an Ace-Queen doubleton in spades and your partner holds a King-Jack doubleton in spades. The contract is no trump, and your matching high cards are wasted)

ENCOURAGE: When a high card (eight and up) is played under your partner's high card lead, which requests him/her to continue the suit.

ENDPLAY: A strategic maneuver in which an opponent is thrown into the lead at the end of a hand, and is forced to make a favorable return to your hand.

ENTRY: Any card which allows access to your partner's hand.

ESTABLISH: To set up or promote winning tricks by driving out key high cards in the opponents' hands.

EXIT: A maneuver to get out of the lead by playing a losing card.

FINESSE: An attempt to win a trick with a lesser or lower card in the same suit.

FIT: The favorable number of cards in the same suit held by both members of a partnership. Also describes the combination of multiple suits between both members of a partnership.

FOLLOW(ING): Describes the play of a card in the same suit led.

GAME: This term has several definitions: The exact number of points required to win a match. A specific number of tricks needed for a particular bid. The variation in effect ("Straight," "Jokers," etc.) A style of play or system used by a partnership.

HAND: Another term for a deal, or the cards held by a specific player.

HESITATION: An unethical or deceptive practice of intentionally delaying the play of a card in order to convey information to one's partner (sometimes called "hitching").

HIGH: The outstanding or winning card of a suit. Also describes a variation of the game (see "Uptown").

HONOR CARD: The A – K – Q – J – 10 of any suit.

HOUSE RULE: Another term for the format or variation of the game. It applies to bidding, scoring, use of Jokers, and sporting of the kitty ("House" is usually a term applied to a casino)

INSUFFICIENT BID: A call or bid that is not legally high enough to outrank or overcall the previous bid.

JOKER: Any additional card or cards added to the deck in order. to create a new variation or extra trump. Jokers are the highest-ranking trump and are "Big" (high) and "Little" (second high).

KITTY: Depending on the use of Jokers, the remaining four, five, or six cards which are separate from those dealt to the players. The kitty (sometimes called the 'Widow") goes to the highest bidder, who has the option to replace less desirable cards in his/her hand.

LAYDOWN: A declaration that a hand is "ice cold," and cannot be defeated (see "Claim").

LEAD: The first card played to any trick or the opening play of the hand.

LHO/RHO: "Left-hand Opponent"/"Right-hand Opponent."

LITTLE: The term for the small Joker, the second highest trump.

LIMIT (GAME): A designated number of points for a game, usually seven, 14, or 21 points.

LONG: Holding great length in any suit. (E.g., Ace, King, xxxx is referred to as "Ace-King sixth.").

LOW: A general term for a losing card in a suit. Also describes a variation of the game (see "Downtown").

MAKE (MAKING): A term describing a successful bid or fulfillment of the required number of tricks.

MAJOR SUITS: Hearts and Spades

MASTER TRUMP: The highest or outstanding remaining card in the trump suit after a few rounds have been played.

MINOR SUITS: Diamonds and Clubs

MISDEAL: A faulty number of cards dealt to a player or to the kitty.

MORALS (AND ETHICS): Another term for honest or "fair" play (see "Cheating").

NO TRUMP: A bid or contract in which the high card wins, and there is no trump suit. Jokers are not used.

ON THE MONEY (ON TIME): Making a bid or contract with the exact number of tricks required.

OPENING BID: Initial bid made by the person to the left of the dealer.

OPENING LEAD: The play of the first card of the hand by the highest bidder (declarer).

OVERTRICK: One book or trick in excess of the designated number required.

PACK: The deck of cards

PASS: No bid, or the choice not to bid.

PENALTY: Points lost for rule or procedural violations.

REVOKE: Failure to follow suit whenever possible. Often referred to as "renege," and is a penalty situation.

RISE AND FLY: A tournament style, featuring a one-hand format, in which the winner of that hand stays at that table and the loser must vacate.

RUFF: Another word for trumping. NOTE: *overruff* refers to playing a higher trump after a ruff; *underruff* refers to discarding or unblocking a lower trump after a ruff.

RUFF/SLUFF: The lead of a suit in which both opponents are void. The result is usually a discard of a losing card by one opponent, as the other trumps. This is considered one of the worst plays in the game.

SACRIFICE: A strategic bid with a risk factor in order to prevent the opponents from winning a game or scoring a slam.

SECOND HAND LOW: The practice of playing a low card in the second position after the lead of a low card. This allows your partner to have the opportunity to win the trick in fourth position.

SET: Taking fewer tricks than the number specified (or bid), or defeating the opponent's bid..

SEQUENCE: Two or more "connected" honor cards of the same suit in the same hand (e.g. King, Queen, Jack, Ace-King).

SHIFT: Often called a "switch" and describing the lead of a different suit by the same player.

SIDE SUIT(S): Any or all of the three outstanding suits after trump has been declared.

SIGNAL: Playing a specific card which conveys information to one's partner, usually part of a pre-arranged convention.

SINGLETON: Holding of only one card in a given suit.

SLAM: A term, taken from Bridge, specifying a six- or seven-level bid.

SPORTING: Showing the cards in the kitty to the other players (this is now an obsolete practice).

SQUEEZE: A forced play against an opponent who must guard two or more suits simultaneously, and thus is forced to discard a key card.

STEP-LEVEL BIDDING: Describes a system in which the levels of bidding are separated. There are "Full Step" and "Half Step" systems. (Each event uses their own system).

STOPPER: Any card which prevents a suit from playing out

TABLE TALK: Jargon for any conversation, body language, or mannerisms with the purpose of conveying information to one's partner. It is considered very unethical and gauche.

THIRD HAND HIGH: The standard play of your highest card in the third position in order to prevent the fourth player from winning a trick with a low card.

TRICK: A book or packet of four cards.

TRUMP: The highest ranking suit. This term is also applied to the play of a trump.

TRUMP PROMOTION: The natural progression of a lower ranking trump to a higher position in the same hand. This is accomplished by a series of ruffs and/or overruffs.

TRUMP REMOVAL or EXTRACTION: Drawing all the trump not held by the declarer's team. Often referred to as "Getting the kids off the street!"

UPPERCUT: Playing a higher trump after an opponent's trump

UPTOWN: A type of contract in which high cards win. Cards are ranked: A, K, Q, J, etc. Jokers, when used, are ranked higher than the trump Ace.

VOID: Holding no cards in a given suit.

WALKING: A slang term describing a particular card winning a trick, especially if a higher card in the same suit 'is not played (sometimes called "skating").

Appendix B

LAWS OF WHIST

NOTE: This is general information; many organizations have created their own laws and game rules tailored specifically for their events / tournaments.

1. Number Of Players:

Whist is a partnership game, with four players seated at a table. Members of a partnership are positioned opposite each other. Each team may be selected by draw of cards, or by pm-arrangement. Two- and three-handed variations do exist, but are strictly for recreational games.

2. The Pack/Variations:

The game of Whist is played with a standard deck of 52 cards with the option of two Jokers. -There are four basic variations:

    a. Bid Whist with a Kitty and two Jokers
    b. Bid Whist with a Kitty and no Jokers
    c. Bid Whist with no Kitty and no Jokers ("Straight")
    d. Non—Bid Whist with no Kitty and no Jokers (obsolete) (bottom card is trump)

A number of other local and regional variations do exist, as well as modifications to any of the above.

3. Ranking of Cards

a. Uptown (High) Bids: A, K, Q, J, 10, 9, 8, 7, 6, 5, 4, 3, 2
b. Downtown (Low) Bids: A, 2, 3, 4, 5, 6, 7, 8, 9, 10, J, Q, K

Options: Jokers ("Big" and "Little") rank above the Ace of trump in suit contracts only. Other cards may also be designated as additional high trump. Jokers are not used in no trump contracts.

4. The Shuffle, Cut, and Deal

These are standard procedures, and have been reviewed previously.

5. Object of the Game

The object of the game of Whist is to win as many books (tricks) as possible in order to fulfill bids (contracts). Points are awarded for successful completion of bids. Points are deducted for unsuccessful ("set") contracts. The standard game ends when a partnership has scored plus seven or minus seven. Other scoring limits may be mutually agreed upon.

6. Bidding

There is one round of bidding, starting to the left of the dealer. Suits are not mentioned. Direction (Uptown or Downtown) is stated. The bid of no trump is also an option. The dealer has the last bid.

7. The Kitty

The highest bidder (declarer) wins the kitty, a separate pack of four, five, or six cards. An equal number of cards must be discarded from the declarer's hand in order to reduce to twelve cards. The kitty is considered the first book for the offense. Some variations of the game are without a kitty, in which case each player has 13 cards.

8. Opening Lead

The highest bidder (declarer) has the first or opening lead of each hand. He/she detaches one card from his/her hand, and places it face up on the table.

9. The Play

After the opening lead, each player in clockwise rotation detaches a card from his/her hand, and places it face up on the table. The four cards, thus played constitute a book or trick. A player must follow suit, if possible. If void of the suit led, said player may "trump" (in suit contracts), or discard any other card. Any card which is placed face up on the table is considered "boarded" (played), and may not be retracted except to correct a revoke. If any card is exposed or played in a manner which clearly indicates an intention to play said card, this constitutes a completed action. The winner of the previous book now leads the first card of the next book. Play proceeds until all 12 cards have been exhausted, one at a time, from each player's hand.

10. Scoring

At the conclusion of a hand, the number of tricks taken are determined for each team. Points are then transcribed to the scoresheet. (Refer to the previous chapter regarding the calculation of points).

11. The Revoke (Renege):

If a player discards when able to follow suit, he/she is said to *renounce.* There is no penalty if the renounce is corrected *before* any card is played to the *next* trick. However, if the trick involving the renounce is completed, *and* a card has been played to the next trick, the renounce now becomes a revoke. The penalty for a revoke is the loss of three tricks to the offending side. The director must determine if a revoke has caused additional damage, and - may award an adjusted score.

12. Claims And Concessions

If a player exposes his/her hand and claims all remaining tricks, he/she must announce the order of play. If this is not done, then either opponent may direct how the cards are to be played. The Director may be called to resolve any dispute.

It is strongly advised to play all hands to a conclusion.

13. Irregularities:

a. **Lead Out of Turn:** If the wrong player leads prematurely or incorrectly, the director must be called. The lead may be accepted by either opponent, in which case, there is no penalty. Or the lead may revert to the proper position, in which case there is a penalty card application.

b. **Bid Out of Turn:** The bid is voided, and the auction resumes to its normal position. In addition, the director has the right to make a ruling if it is determined that information from the incorrect bid affected the result of the hand. Repeated violations will be penalized with the loss of a point for each infraction.

c. **Exposed/Penalty Card:** Any card prematurely exposed during the play of the hand, as part of lead out of turn or a renounce, is deemed as a penalty card. This card will remain face up in front of the offender, and must be played at the first legal opportunity. If information from the exposed card is deemed to be damaging to the opponents, the director has the right to make an appropriate ruling.

14. Ethics/ Kibitzer's Rights

The rules/procedures coordinator of any club or tournament has the right to establish guidelines for each event.

While it is recognized that the game of Whist does have some tradition, there must be protocol as well. Here are some issues to be addressed:

1. Blatant table talk
2. Excessive body language
3. Profanity
4. Criticism of opponents or partner
5. Unwillingness to accept decision of director
6. Cheating (and accusations of same)

In addition, boundaries must established for Kibitzers (spectators). Issues to be considered are:

1. Showing emotion or facial expression at any time
2. Making comments during the bidding
3. "Coaching" or giving advice to any player
4. Examining the kitty
5. Taking a side during an argument or discussion
6. Bringing attention to any violation of rules

Whist has been around for hundreds of years, and will outlast all of us. Let's have fun at the table, and enjoy this wonderful classic game.

Dennis Jerome Barmore

1950–2008

BY JOE ANDREWS, 2009

I MET DENNIS BARMORE on a Caribbean card game cruise in the Summer of 2000. He was hosting Bid Whist, and I was hosting Spades tournaments while the ship was "at sea" between port stops. I was very impressed with his outgoing and congenial personality. We started talking about my Grand Prix "live" events, and its formats / rules for Spades, Hearts and Euchre, and the multiple round qualifiers. Soon thereafter, he decided to organize and launch a National Series for the game of Bid Whist. It was to be known as "National Card Sharks" a/k/a " The Bid Whist Across America Tour". I had the opportunity to attend several of his 'first year" Eastern U.S. regular tournaments, as well as two special events - one in Las Vegas (with Darryl Mobley & Family Digest Magazine,) and one in Los Angeles (with Steve Harvey). The latter was held at the Palladium and featured Bid Whist, Spades, Dominoes, and Chess! I was able to arrange a sponsorship with the U.S. Playing Card Company (Bicycle Cards) for the new Series.

As the years went by, we maintained our friendship, and I also had the opportunity to meet several of his tournament players and hosts. The "Sharks" events were always well — organized, and a lot of Prize money was won. The web site www.sharksinc.com was a labor of love for Dennis, and the pictures / statistics were always up to date. The

Atlanta events became legendary for their huge turnouts! And I will never forget his first Las Vegas National Tournament of Champions at the Plaza Hotel ! The years passed. Occasionally, our paths would cross at the hotels where "Grand Prix" and "Sharks" events would be sharing the same hotel facilities. And it was always great seeing my friends from the early days of the tournaments. I heard about Dennis Barmore's passing in May of 2008.

It was a sad day for the entire Bid Whist community, and the many legions of friends and admirers who will always remember this wonderful man.

Here is a brief history of National Card Sharks by Dennis Barmore:

"We may not be the NFL or the NBA; we may not make millions of dollars a year like Pro basketball players, but we do compete for thousands of dollars a month on:
"THE BID WHIST ACROSS AMERICA TOUR"

Attention - All Bid Whist Players:

"The National Card Sharks was formed on September 12, 1980 at the Gatsby Nightclub in Baltimore Maryland. That night and the following night we held tournaments in Bid Whist, Single Deck Pinochle, and Double Deck Pinochle. We then began to run one night tournaments and 16 week leagues in a multitude of night clubs and some malls in the Baltimore area. We were running leagues at least 3 nights a week. In 1983 we began to venture up and down the East Coast challenging cities to meet and compete against us. We accomplished this by placing newspaper ads in cities such as Philadelphia, New York, and Richmond. In the ads , we would say that The National Card Sharks were coming to their city, and we will be playing at a certain location, and we invite all interested local players to participate With the invention of the Internet in the late 1980's, we were able to issue that challenge across the USA at practically no cost. We also encouraged players from cities across the USA to form Bid Whist and Pinochle clubs in their area. In 2001 we launched what would become 'The Bid Whist Across America Tour". It started with tournaments in Atlanta and Las Vegas. In 2002 we traveled to eight cities, and since 2003 we have expanded the tour to ten cities.

The game of Bid whist is one of the truly African American pastimes. It is much too important to African American culture to let die. Please tell all of your friends and relatives about us, and to help is keep Bid Whist alive."

After his passing in 2008, these live Bid Whist events were renamed CardSharksinc.

"Nessie", "Lenora", and "Tiffany" become the Directors and organizers of the Tournaments. In addition, there were coordinators appointed to help with the East and West Coast Regions. An annual national qualifying series of Tournaments in various cities was also scheduled. This culminated in the National Championship event in Las Vegas, NV.

A CardSharksinc Educational Fund was established. Each year, different recipients are chosen. To date, the Dennis J. Barmore Foundation has awarded several College scholarships. This is a fitting tribute to the memory of Mr. Barmore.

Official Rules
For Bid Whist Tournaments

Card Sharks Inc. Official Rules

Bid Whist With Kitty And Jokers

Teams will play a 1 round game (4 hands) to determine the Elite 8 teams. The winners of the Elite 8 round are paired off via the bracket, in a 1 round game to become The Final Four. The Final Four are paired off via the bracket. Then the winners of the Final Four pairings play for 1st & 2nd Place, and the losers of the Final Four parings play for 3rd & 4th Place.

General Rules for Frequently Asked Questions
- The Guarantee Joker is the little joker.
- No Sporting the kitty.

- You cannot count your partners kitty.
- Minimum bid is 4.
- If you bid a 7 NO, you can state your direction and pick up the kitty with out waiting for other players to pass.
- Pay Attention — No bid whist talking after play begins. You cannot ask what the trump card is, what card led, or who played what, after the 1st card has been played to the board. (You may look at the scoresheet to review the bid).
- You may ask the bidder to repeat a bid before play begins.
- Bid blinds, when available, will be used for the Sweet 16, and Final Rounds. The blind will go up after all cards are dealt and before any bids are placed.

2. The Deal

When the round begins, the person that draws the first diamond becomes the first dealer. Cards are shuffled (face down only). Player to the right of (behind) the dealer cuts the cards at least once and no more than twice. Dealer deals cards to the left one at a time in a clockwise order. Each player is to receive 12 cards for a total of 48 cards, and 6 cards are put in a kitty. The kitty may not consist of the first four or the last four cards dealt. Do not put more than one card in the kitty at a time. (No consecutive cards in the kitty). Do not pick up your cards until it is your turn to bid.

3. Bidding

The bidding goes around the table only once starting with the player to the left of the dealer. The bid may range from 4 — 7 points. When you bid, designate your bid clearly. You cannot change your bid. State your bid and place your cards back on the table until the first card is played. Be sure to count your cards before playing the hand. Standard bids should be used as follows:

- Four, Five, Six, Seven - Means you intend to name a trump, and that high cards will win.

- Four Special, Five Special, Six Special, Seven Special - Means that you intend to name a trump, and low cards will win.
- Four No, Five No, Six No, Seven No - Means that there will be no trump named, and that if you win the bid you will determine if high or low cards will have preference.

NOTE: The following bids are examples of bids that should not be used:

- "Four High"
- "Five Low"
- Knocking on the table, "You Can Have It", "Bye me", "I pass"
- "Five No Trump"

Bids with trumps: When you attempt a bid with trumps, you indicate the direction you are bidding. You do not name which suit you intend to name as trumps, until you win the bid. Bidding is progressive. This means that a 'Special' bid does not take out "High" bid. Only a No bid can take out a trump bid of the same number of books.

Rank of Trumps: The priority of the trump suit is as follows.

- High Bids with Trumps - Big Joker, Little Joker (Guarantee), A,K,Q,J,10,9,8,7,6,5,4,3,2
- "Special" Bids with Trumps - Big Joker, Little Joker (Guarantee), A,2,3,4,5,6,7,8,9,10,J,Q,K for a low bid.

Bids without trumps: A No bid takes out a trump bid of the same number. (Example: if I bid a 4, a 4 special bid does not supersede me, but a 4 No or any number above 4 with or without trumps does supersede me.) When bidding a No bid, you do not indicate which direction (uptown or downtown), until you win the bid. In a no bid the jokers are nil, (of no value, cannot win a book.) and must be played the first time that you do not have any cards of the suit led.

Failure to do so results in a renege. In the event the joker is the only remaining card in your hand, the suit of the player to the left determines the play.

The Kitty: 6 card kitty. Once every player has bid, the winner may pick up and discard the kitty. The discarded kitty should remain with the bidder. Do not sport the kitty. All books collected during hand play should be placed on the same side of the table.

Rank of Bids: The priority of wining the bidding process is as follows. (Starting with the lowest bid possible, to the highest bid possible.)

- 4 or 4 Special
- 4 No
- 5 or 5 Special
- 5 No
- 6 or 6 Special
- 6 No
- 7 or 7 Special
- 7 No

4. Play of Hand

Once the bid is won and the player has discarded 6 cards for their kitty, the bidder should ensure the bid was recorded properly by the scorekeeper. Play begins with the player winning the bid leading out with the first card. If bid blinds are in effect, the blind goes down.

With Trumps Hand: A trump always wins the book. If there is more than one trump played, then the highest or lowest ranking trump based on the type of bid taken will win the book. If no trumps are played, then the highest or lowest ranking card to the suit led wins the book. Players must follow suit, if they have it in their hand. If a suit is led and the player does not have that suit in their hand then that player has the option to play a trump or play a different suit.

No Trump Hand: In a No Trump hand, the highest or lowest ranking card to the suit led wins the book. If the bidding team makes the No Trump bid double points are earned, if the bidding team does not make the No trump bid, the opposing team earns double-points. **Scoring by Hands.** At the end of the hand (all cards are played), the bidding team must count their books and have to make at least as many points as their bid or they will be set (loose the hand). If the bid is set, the opposing team will be awarded the points of their bid. The opposing team cannot make odds on a bid. If the bid is made, the bidding team wins the points that they actually made, which may exceed the amount they bid.

5. *Scoring by Rounds*

At the end of the 4th hand, the total scores earned for the 4 hands are added and the winner of that round is determined by the highest score. (Example: If on the first hand your team just makes their 4 No bid, your team earns 8 points. Please note that the game is not over because you still have 3 hands remaining in the round.) The winner of the round is not determined until all 4 hands are played except in Sweet 16 and Final Rounds.

TieBreaker: If each team has earned the same number of points, a tiebreaker hand will be played to determine the winner of that round. Note: Points earned in the tiebreaker hand will not count toward the team's total score. The tiebreaker hand is only used to determine the winner of that particular round.

6. *Renege (Loss of Bid)*

A team cannot call a renege on themselves, only the opposing team can call a renege. Once the book is turned, it cannot be viewed, unless a renege is called. A book is considered turned when a book has been turned over, removed from playing area, and placed face down. A player should not attempt to turn a book until each player has played a card.

A renege or error can be caused by the following:

- If a player fails to follow suit when they have a card of that suit in their hand.
- A player plays a trump on a led suit that the player has in their hand.
- A player bids out of turn
- A player plays out of turn
- Pay attention and play the right card the first time, you cannot put back a card in your hand, once it is exposed.
- A player talks bid whist across the board or to anyone else during bidding and play.
- Note: If a player makes an improper bid, they must bid the next higher number. Example: if a player bids a 4 Special after a 4 bid, that player must bid the 5 Special. A player cannot change their bid (direction, between trump or no trump.)
- In a No hand, a player fails to play a joker the first time a suit is led which they do not have in their hand.
- Exposed cards during play or while setting the kitty

Players must pay Attention! Players cannot ask what trump is, what led, or who played what, after the 1st card has been played to the board. (A player may ask to look at the scoresheet to view the bid).

The tournament director is the final authority on all rulings & disputes. In some cases these rules may seem harsh to the casual player, but remember, you're in a tournament now!

THE COLUMBUS WHIST PLAYERS SOCIETY

www.columbuswhist.com

Club History

The Columbus Whist Players Society, the First, originated through a vision of people, with like interests and passionate about playing the game known as "Straight" Bid Whist, in Columbus, Ohio and its neighboring cities. Bid Whist is a partnership trick-taking game that is very popular among African Americans.

In 1994, after years of playing at each other's homes, local bars, and using other organizations facilities, these same people decided to pursue the ultimate dream of having our own clubhouse. We established a dues paying membership of over 50 people, created our Mission Statement, the Club's purpose and our Constitution and Bylaws. On April 25, 1995, we registered, with State of Ohio, and became chartered, on 05/16/1995, as a not for profit organization.

In late 1999, an opportunity to have our own place, presented itself, and needless to say, the members at that time, did not hesitate to pursue our dream. The place was a store front warehouse, located in an industrial area, with nothing but cement floors and concrete walls. We moved in, painted the walls, installed carpeting, light fixtures, purchased storage cabinets, refrigerators, tables and chairs, hung pictures and had the nicest restrooms for both the men and women. This was all done with cash and donations made from the members. After a couple hot summers of using fans, the members decided to have central air installed and once again, paid cash. It was such a nice feeling to know that we had some place nice to go and invite others to join us now to play cards.

As people started hearing about us, our membership continued to grow and we began to meet a lot of good people, mostly claiming to be experts in the playing whist. We were always able to show them where the best card players really lived

We started having weekly and monthly tournaments at our own place. CWPS holds Bid Whist Leagues and Champ of Champ tournaments annually. We held our 1st Annual Statewide Tournaments on October 17, 1998, 6 cards Kitty and No Kitty. Today, our "Statewide" tournaments are 2 days and consist of a total of 4 tournaments. We certainly have come a long way. We owe this growth to traveling and competing throughout the nation in other organizations' tournaments.

CWPS has always been known for our unique style of play in straight whist (now known as No Joker, No Kitty). Our game is: 5 and out, 2 sets and odd paper. We decided to seek other cities that like playing bid whist, without a kitty. It didn't take long to identify those cities and establish a traveling group willing to play and compete with straight whist being the only game of choice. Today those other cities are; Chicago, Illinois and Detroit, Michigan. Our organization is called the "No Kitty Coalition" and our tournaments are called "City to City — No Kitty" and we hold (3) tournaments in one day, in each city, annually. We kicked off our 1st stop in Columbus, Ohio, hosted by the CWPS, on Saturday, April 30, 2011. The 2nd stop was hosted by the Top of the World Bid Whist & Social Club, in Chicago, Illinois, on Saturday, June 25, 2011 and last stop was hosted by the Motor City Whist Mechanics, in Detroit, Michigan, on September 10, 2011. We are proud to announce, we are in our 3rd year and this organization is growing. This also means "No Kitty" bid whist is growing. This is another milestone.

In late 2011, a few members of CWPS wanted to learn how to play pinochle so we started looking for those who played. We made contact with the president of Bucks and Doe Pinochle Club, Columbus' local chapter of the National Pinochle Association (NPA) and members of the Retired Air Force Association (RAFA). As the relationships grew, so did the interest of learning how to play pinochle. CWPS now has a pinochle day on Tuesdays. As of June 12, 2012, we held our 1st pinochle tournament. We now have Active and Guest members who are pinochle players. Another milestone accomplished.

On October 18, 2012, CWPS started an outreach program, at Summit's Trace Healthcare Center, with the intention of hosting Bid Whist card parties at their facility, quarterly. Our ultimate goal is to start a senior day care, to be located at our own clubhouse, every Monday and Thursday.

CWPS Purpose and Mission

Purpose: To play and enjoy the games of whist and pinochle in an informal atmosphere of friendship, mutual respect fair play and healthy competition.

Mission: To continue and advance interest in learning and playing whist, the forerunner of bridge, by playing and coaching to improve the play of whist and pinochle for fun and tournament competition. To continue our involvement with community activities, provide annual food baskets and yearly donations to charitable causes.

Special thanks to Phyllis Cornute
for the CWPS history and information.

NO KITTY-NO JOKER
CARD PLAYING RULES

Format

1. The game will be played without a kitty.
2. 6 games will be played.
3. 5 points positive or negative is game.
4. The tournament officials will determine the number of teams who will advance to the playoff round based on the number of teams participating in the tournament. The most games won will determine which teams advance.
5. Points are awarded for the number of books made.
6. Points are only used in the event of ties. If there are ties, there will be a one game play-off. Points are of no value in the one game playoff.
7. 2 sets (bad bids) are game regardless of the score.
8. If a game is won by 2 sets (bad bids), odd, or a renege, the opposing team will receive 5 additional points.
9. If a game is won on the first hand by the non-bidding team, they will receive 5 points.
10. *5-minute rule. If you are not in your seat ready to play within 5 minutes at the start of a game, the opposing team will be awarded the game and will receive 5 points.

Deal

11. The first club will determine who deals first. The deal proceeds clockwise.
12. The deck *MUST* be cut before each deal begins and the deck must remain face down on the table. Multiple cuts are allowed.
13. If any card is exposed when dealing, there must be a re-deal by the correct person.
14. It is a misdeal if the wrong player dealt. The hand is void and the correct player must re-deal.
15. *It is a misdeal if any player does not have the correct number of cards before bidding begins. The hand is void and the correct player must re-deal.
16. You may not pick up your hand until the bid blind is in place.
17. *Once the bid blind goes up, there is absolutely no talking (exceptions — see rules #18, 19, 20, 22, 23, 25, 29, 30, 31, 32, 35, 37 and 38).
18. The first card played signals when the bid blind comes down and before the next card is played. If the next card is played before the bid blind comes down, the other players have a right to ask who played what card only.
19. If a card is exposed after the deal is done but before bidding begins, the opposing team has the option to continue play or re-deal.

Bid

20. *All players must count their cards before they make a bid. If you are short of cards or have extra cards, the hand is void and the correct player must re-deal.
21. *The minimum bid is 1.
22. *All bidding must be verbal. The only acceptable bids are for example, pass, 1, 1 special or 1 no. You cannot say no-trump. If you say the word "trump", the opposing team has the option to continue play or re-deal.

23. *No player may drag their bid (no half-stepping). For example, the bidder says 3; pauses and then says special. If this happens, the opposing team has the option to continue play or re-deal.*

No Kitty-No Joker Card Playing Rules

24. *Progressive bidding. Each bid must be at least one number higher <u>than</u> the previous bid, except for a "no" bid. No player may make a bid that is not progressive or that gives inappropriate information. If this happens, that bidder is forced to make the progressive bid; their partner is silenced and cannot bid.

25. *If a player bids out of turn, the opposing team has the option to let the bid stand or re-deal. If the bid stands, the opposing team can still bid. However, the person who made the infraction; their partner is silenced and cannot bid.

26. If all players pass, the dealer must bid a minimum of 2, 2 special or 2 no.

27. The person awarded the bid must name a trump or the first card played is automatically trump (exception see #28).

28. *If the bidder bids a "no" then plays a card without stating the direction of the bid, the opposing team will be awarded the game and 5 points.

Play

29. *All cards must remain in your hands during play. If a player exposes their cards at any time after all bids are made, to include playing out of turn, it is an automatic set for their team for the points of the bid regardless of who bids *UNLESS* the opposing team wants to continue play. If you already have a set (bad bid), it is game. If the bid is a one (of any kind), a set is odd; it is game and the opposing team will be awarded 5 points.

30. Once play starts, if the bidding team is short of cards or has extra cards, the bidding team is set for the points of the bid.
31. Once play starts if the non-bidding team is short of cards or has extra cards, the bidding team has the option to continue play or take the points of the bid.
32. *Once play starts if a player from each team is short of cards or has extra cards, the hand is void and the correct player must re-deal.
33. Each team must keep their books together in one straight line on one side of the table.
34. The team collecting the books must allow all 4 cards to be seen before turning the book over.
35. Once the book is turned over, it is a closed book and may not be re-opened *UNLESS* you are calling a renege. Books must be turned over by a tournament director.
36. A team calling a renege may do so at anytime and a tournament director must be called before going through any books, the books must be turned over by a tournament director.
37. Each book must be closed before the correct player leads the next card.
38. All hands must be played out regardless of the score *UNLESS* all players agree to stop play. Any infraction, the exposed card rule (#29) applies.
39. *If there is a Boston pot, the team with the most Boston's by the 4th game wins. If the Boston pot is not hit by the 4th game, the team with the best record wins. If more than one team has the best record, the pot will be split equally among those teams.
40. All scores are final when the score sheet is signed by both teams. No changes will be made.

If a player leaves before completing play and they do not have a substitute player, their team forfeits all remaining games and their money will not be refunded.

A tournament director must be called for any ruling and their ruling is final!!!!!!

HISTORY OF
DUPLICATE WHIST

By John Gouveia, Director of the Taunton, MA Whist Club

"Before there was Bridge (early 1900's), there was Whist. And before there was duplicate Bridge, there was duplicate Whist. Those who have played the modern game duplicate Bridge will be familiar with what are known as duplicate Bridge trays or boards. They are trays with slots, usually made of aluminum today, which contain the hands that are to be played in the typical tournament. The idea to eliminate the luck of the deal, and to gain a true comparison of those who play the same hands in the same direction. The concept works well for Whist, Spades, Pinochle, or any card game played with a Partner.

Duplicate Whist was invented in London in 1857 by Henry Jones AKA "Cavendish". It was developed as a refined version of the game by eliminating the luck of the draw making it more of a skills competition. The 1st duplicate whist game in the U.S. was played privately in Chicago in 1880 and in a club in New Orleans in 1882. The first interclub match was played in Philadelphia in 1883. The first duplicate match in Europe was in Glasgow, Scotland, in 1888.

Major steps in the progression of the game came in 1891 with the foundation of the American Whist League; the invention of the Kalamazoo tray (first duplicate board); and the first book on tournament organization, written by John T. Mitchell who devised the first movement for pair play (North & South), and the method of pointing which has been used ever since.

Duplicate Whist became the primary game played in the Whist Clubs and at tournaments through the turn of the century up to the 1920'sMost cities and major universities had Whist Clubs that regularly engaged in competitions.

Although the American Whist League was to flourish for some 40 years; it succumbs to Duplicate Bridge as the game played in the Clubs.

Henry Jones A.K.A. "Cavendish"
Inventor of Duplicate Whist

Even though Duplicate Whist was replaced by Bridge in the clubs, it was still played in some circles up to and beyond the early 1940's.

The Monday Team Whist Club of Lawrence, Kansas an all women's club founded in 1901 started playing Duplicate Whist in 1904 and is the longest running Duplicate Whist game on record playing privately in homes right up to 1966.

Classic Whist (non-duplicate) style charity whist parties were legalized in the state of MA in 1932 and most Catholic Churches and Social Clubs held Whist Parties playing 25 or more hands of whist for prizes along with side raffles and bake sales. These whist parties were used as a major fundraising mechanism due to the fact that Bingo or Beano was banned in the State Massachusetts in 1943 per an emergency order which read "The manner in which the games of beano have been and are conducted in many parts of the Commonwealth has been and is detrimental to the public welfare" as then declared by Governor Leveret Saltonsall. Whist party popularity continued right through the 1950's and 1960's with many weekly game held regularly. Special games, such as a Turkey Whist were a popular attraction during Thanksgiving time. These parties continued to be profitable up to time when Bingo was once again legalized in the State of Massachusetts and put under the direction of the State Lottery Commission in 1973 and thus Bingo became the game of choice for fundraising.